Heading
for Victory

Heading for Victory

an autobiography

STEVE BRUCE

BLOOMSBURY

First published in Great Britain 1994
Bloomsbury Publishing Limited, 2 Soho Square, London W1V 5DE
Copyright 1994 by Steve Bruce

The moral right of the author has been asserted

PICTURE SOURCES
Newcastle Chronicle: pages 1 *bottom*, 2 *bottom*
South Eastern Newspapers Ltd: page 3 *bottom*
Bob Thomas: pages 4 *top*, 5, 7, 9 *bottom*
Allsport UK Ltd: pages 12 *bottom*, 13, 14, 15, 16
Remaining pictures from Steve Bruce

A CIP catalogue record for this book is available
from the British Library

ISBN 0 7475 17800

10 9 8 7 6 5 4 3 2 1

Typeset by Hewer Text Composition Services, Edinburgh
Printed in England by Clays Ltd, St Ives Plc

For my mum, dad, Janet, Alex and Amy

Chapter One

Only three men this century have known the feeling I experienced at Wembley Stadium on Saturday, May 14th, 1994. Those other three have been Danny Blanchflower, Frank McLintock and Alan Hansen. What is the link? We have all been captains of sides that have achieved the double of winning both the championship and the FA Cup in the same season. Tottenham did it in 1961 to prove that it was possible in the modern game; ten years later, Arsenal emulated their North London rivals; and Liverpool managed to do it in 1986. Whatever else they accomplished in the game, the moment marked a pinnacle in the careers of those other captains. When I went up those famous steps to the Royal Box to receive the Cup from the Duchess of Kent, having picked up the Premiership trophy a week earlier, I could not help but feel just a tinge of disappointment that we had missed out. We had come so close to doing something that has never been done before – and perhaps never will. Manchester United came within a match of completing the treble.

It seems ridiculous to confess that we considered the double to be something of a consolation prize: we genuinely believed that we were good enough to make a clean sweep of all the domestic trophies on offer. It was ironic that we were prevented from doing so by Aston Villa, the same club that had prevented Manchester United from achieving the most formidable challenge in football, when they had walked out for the FA Cup Final with the League title already secured, in 1957.

Apart from that one slight regret regarding the treble, it

1

was a fantastic season for us. By winning the double, we had accomplished even more than the Busby Babes and famous team players such as Charlton, Law and Best. Furthermore, we had done it with a style that would not have disgraced our celebrated predecessors who have worn the famous red shirt. That has always been important to us at Old Trafford, and it was fitting that, in the year of Sir Matt Busby's passing, we should have achieved so much in a manner that would have satisfied him.

We took great delight in the praise we received from ordinary football fans, who said how much they enjoyed the way we played and thanked us for the entertainment we had given them. On the other hand, we did object to the damning criticism over a couple of isolated incidents. I know that when you are up at the top you are in the shooting-line, but I could not understand why some people did not just offer criticism, and instead took delight in what was no more than a cheap knocking. The fact that some people seemed determined to look for trifling faults only served to stiffen our resolve to succeed.

I feel privileged to be part of a great side and a wonderful club. Every football-mad boy dreams that one day he will collect trophies and play at Wembley. In these last few years, I have had to pinch myself to make sure that I am not still a kid on Tyneside imagining it all. The enjoyment and satisfaction obtained from our success is only heightened by the fact that it has not come easily for me. I found it difficult to break into the game, and then served a hard apprenticeship in the lower divisions. If I had my dreams like everyone else, there were times when I thought they would be no more than that. There was a long way to go before the day when I showed the FA Cup to the world as confirmation that I was captain of the Manchester United side that had just done the double. It was, however, something which had always appeared possible after we had made the breakthrough in winning the League title a year earlier.

After that success, we reported back for the 1993–94

season in a confident frame of mind. It is fair to say that the celebrations had never really stopped, and it enabled us to virtually pick up from where we had left off. The people of Manchester never ceased to express their congratulations and pleasure that we had won the title after such a long period, and wherever any of us went, in this country or abroad, we found Manchester United supporters who insisted that the party atmosphere continue.

As every season dawns there is the hope that the next campaign is going to be more successful than the last. This applies to every club, whether they have finished top or bottom of the League the previous time. I can clearly remember the bubbling optimism that was around Old Trafford at that time. The pre-season tour to South Africa had been a huge success in every way, and we had won the Charity Shield by beating Arsenal. We not only hoped that we were going to improve on the previous season, we genuinely believed that we would do better. At the same time, we knew that it was going to be harder to retain our title than it had been to win it in the first place. Everyone makes a special effort against the champions and, as everyone likes to beat Manchester United anyway, we were in for a double dose of fervent opposition.

Alex Ferguson had made only one major signing during the closed season, with Roy Keane joining us from Nottingham Forest. Roy is such a talented player that he fitted in immediately. He appeared a good buy from the outset, adding to both the depth and the quality of our squad. His arrival meant that there was even more competition for places, but it is upon such a philosophy that the Club is based. There is never any possibility of a player becoming complacent or believing that his place in the side is assured. Roy had the opportunity to join Blackburn, but decided to come to Old Trafford. That gave us a boost, because it is one thing to be able to afford virtually every quality player who becomes available, but another to actually persuade him to sign.

In addition to the confidence we gained from having won the title, there was a determination to keep our standards up and bring more prestige to the club. Additionally, there was the prospect of playing in the European Cup once again. There is such a long history associating United with this competition that we could not wait to get back into action in Europe's premier club competition. We had a taste of what it was all about by winning the Cup-winners' Cup in 1991. Now we wanted to prove ourselves at an even higher level. Everything was set for a momentous season.

It began at Norwich, which is always a special match for me, having spent a very happy spell of my career with the Norfolk Club. It is never an easy game there because they are well-organised, and at the time they had a particularly good management team in Mike Walker and John Deehan. They had done their homework well. For the first of what turned out to be many occasions during the season, they refused to come to play against us and merely tried to contain us. It has been a growing trend, with teams worried about the pace we have in the wide positions. Norwich presented us with the first example of a team playing with a sweeper and still keeping two wide defenders to prevent themselves from becoming exposed to one of our major strengths. Despite this, we won 2–0, thanks to a first-half goal from Ryan Giggs, with Bryan Robson adding another in the second half. We were on our way.

Sheffield United were our first opponents at Old Trafford when Roy Keane endeared himself to the home fans with two goals in a 3–0 victory. It was just the sort of start we wanted, because we were playing some terrific football, winning, and had yet to concede a goal. That record fell in our next match, at home to Newcastle, when my home-town club not only held us to a draw, but the phenomenal Andy Cole set off on his goal-scoring spree for the season. There was no doubt that he was destined to become a top-class striker the way he played against us that day.

Another quality player came back into the first team

starting line-up for the game against Aston Villa: Lee Sharpe returned for what must have rated as one of the most entertaining matches of the season to score twice. Numerous people have said how much they enjoyed a game which could have gone either way. There is always the likelihood of a memorable encounter with Villa, for Ron Atkinson usually brings the best out of his teams to play us. He usually has good footballing sides playing open football, even if, on this occasion, Villa also played with a deep defence. It still made for a thrilling encounter, played at a hundred miles an hour. Nobody enjoyed it more than Lee Sharpe who, as a Birmingham lad, took great delight in his double.

It was good to see him back near his best, for he had had a terrible time with illness and injury. There was an occasion when he suffered an attack of meningitis, and thought his footballing days might be over. He awoke in the middle of the night and thought he was suffering from a stroke, and when his parents went to see him, he could not talk properly and just mumbled a few incoherent words. All this, after playing for England as a nineteen-year-old and setting the place alight. We were all devastated when we heard that such a big, strong lad had something like meningitis, but he is a tough character and came back well. He is also well liked by everybody, especially the young girls who follow United! On a more serious note, he is very mature and there is no one better at handling hospital visits and other charity events. It is a great thing to see him behaving so naturally with young children.

Apart from meningitis, Lee Sharpe had also had a couple of hernia problems, so we were all delighted to see him back in action. He scored again as we beat Southampton and in the win against West Ham, when I found the net for the first time. We had played six matches and had sixteen points out of a possible eighteen. It was a more than satisfactory start. That was when we went to Stamford Bridge to meet Chelsea.

A few days later we were due to play our first European

Cup match and the manager decided to experiment with the type of formation we were going to use later in the week. Against Chelsea we employed Roy Keane wide on the right, with neither Mark Hughes nor Andrei Kanchelskis in the line-up. The strict ruling in European competition hits British clubs particularly hard. I think it is nonsense that clubs cannot play at full strength in such an important competition. I am sure that the fans would like to see the players who have won the domestic competition playing in Europe, without Italian clubs having to leave out some of their German and Dutch stars, Spanish clubs losing their South Americans and even us without a full complement of people like Peter Schmeichel, Eric Cantona and Andrei Kanchelskis, or the Welsh, Irish and Scots, all of whom are such an important part of our club. It was a ruling designed to harm British clubs and it would certainly do us no good later in the competition.

That was in the future. In attempting to come to terms with the problem which awaited us at Chelsea, we lost 1–0. I do not think we deserved to lose; Peter Schmeichel would be the first to admit that he should have hung onto the ball, but Gavin Peacock seized on the rebound to score. It was not the ideal preparation for our return to the European Cup in Hungary. Honved were our opponents and, if not one of the great clubs of Europe, the mere fact that we were once again appearing in the Champions' Cup was enough to generate a buzz of excitement. The great team of Best, Charlton and Law had won the League and then gone on to win the European Cup. We had laid one ghost by winning the League; now we wanted to emulate their performance in Europe.

While Honved might not seem to be in the same class as Barcelona, Inter Milan, Real Madrid, AC Milan, Benfica or Ajax, we found that they did have a good record in Europe. Not many teams have gone there and won. We had been seeded to go through to reach at least the mini-League stages of the competition, and thought we were good enough to get there, knowing that it was only two ties away. Honved represented our first test in their stadium in front of one of the great players of a former age, Ferenc Puskas. We got off to a great start, with Roy Keane running them ragged on the right-hand side, so although the strategy might not have worked at Stamford Bridge, it was a resounding success in Budapest. He scored twice and Eric Cantona added another in a 3–2 win. We were coasting through 3–1 before they scored their second about quarter of an hour from the end. It was still a good win, but it would have been that little bit better if they had not been allowed to come back with that second goal.

In the return at Old Trafford, I scored with two headers from corners. I have a reasonable record of scoring in Europe, where perhaps they do not enjoy the idea of a typical English centre half coming up for the set pieces, and adding a physical presence to the attack. This pair gave us a 2–1 win on the night, 5–3 on the aggregate. Between the European matches we beat Arsenal 1–0 in the League, but lost 2–1 to Stoke in a Coca Cola Cup tie with an admittedly weakened side. Alex Ferguson knew it was going to be a long, hard season, so he took this opportunity to play some of the squad players to give regulars a rest. I had suffered a cut head against Arsenal, so I was one of those rested, but I was on the bench and came on for the last fifteen minutes to keep up an appearance record that would not be broken until the League campaign was nearly over. Further League wins against the bottom clubs, Swindon, Sheffield Wednesday and Spurs, followed and we also made up for the Coca Cola cup defeat by beating Stoke 2–0 in the second leg.

In the European Cup we had been paired with the Turkish champions, Galatasaray. We got away to a dream start, with an own goal before Bryan Robson put us 2–0 up within the first fifteen minutes. We were cruising, and perhaps allowed ourselves to get a little slack. A tremendous shot from thirty yards out brought the Turks back to 2–1, and still very much in the tie. Once again, we had to shuffle our side, so it was not the usual defensive formation that got into such a terrible tangle, resulting in Lee Martin virtually putting the ball in his own goal. Now we were desperate, especially when they got another after half time. To be fair, they deserved their lead. We had to rely on a late Eric Cantona goal to give us a life-line at 3–3. We had not played well, we had been a little bit sloppy, but we knew we were capable of going there and getting through. Having let in three goals at home, a draw was unlikely to be any good to us in Turkey. We had to go and win.

In the build-up to that second leg we had three matches in domestic competition to play. We picked up six more League points from matches against Everton and Queens Park Rangers, and had a comfortable 5–1 win over Leicester City in the Coca Cola Cup. In that match I again scored twice. What I would have given for one or both of those goals in Turkey when they were really needed! We also required a full squad to select our team, but unfortunately Gary Pallister was injured. Not only is he a vital member of the side who would have been quite capable of leaving his own defensive duties to upset their defence, but he is also an Englishman. While accepting that it was our own fault that we went there on level terms, we did begin to feel that things were conspiring against us.

Any apprehension we felt before departure was confirmed when we arrived in Turkey. I have played all over the place, but neither I nor any other member of the side had ever experienced anything like the atmosphere in Turkey. We were 'greeted' at the airport by banners carrying the friendly message 'Welcome to Hell!' and from there on the hostility increased. To be fair, our hotel was first-class and we had no complaints there, but that was not the case for many of our supporters. The English football fan may not have a good reputation abroad, but on this occasion they were undoubtedly victimised and treated appallingly. There is no justification for a seventy-five-year-old being woken up in his hotel bedroom and thrown into a prison cell for the duration of his stay in Turkey. That was not an isolated incident. There were too many horror stories to be in any way considered as acceptable behaviour by the authorities.

Our experiences at the match itself were not much better. We could not just go for a walk when we arrived at the stadium an hour and a half before the match. We had to be escorted by the police with riot shields to protect us from coins and other missiles. The match ended disappointingly for us at 0–0, but I am convinced that, had we looked like winning, the match would have been abandoned in a riot. The atmosphere was too intimidating for the home fans to contemplate defeat. The noise and the passion the fans created was unbelievable, and I had no complaint about that in itself. Looking back, it was a fantastic experience, the like of which we will never have to cope with again. It was just that there was a more sinister undertone to proceedings.

Once the final whistle had gone, we had to accept that our dream had gone. We were out of Europe. What we should not have had to accept was the treatment we received as we left the pitch. The police were there, supposedly to protect us, and they were trying to get us away from the home fans by ushering us down the tunnel. In fact, there was not just one tunnel, because as soon as you left the pitch it was like a rabbit warren. At the end of one tunnel was the sanctuary of our dressing room, but before we could reach it, I saw a policeman punch Eric Cantona in the back of the head. That was the signal for Bryan Robson to go to his rescue and, as usual, Bryan came off worse. As he was trying to protect himself and Eric, the policeman lashed out with his riot shield, resulting in Bryan needing stitches in his arm where he had put it up in self defence.

We knew that Europe was the ultimate testing ground for ability and temperament, but this was going too far as a test of character. As well as being disgusted by what had gone on, we were also desperately disappointed. We knew that we should have done better than to go out at the second hurdle, while we felt a little cheated by the 'foreigner' rule. It is not just a whinge, for I really believe it is a bad regulation that deprives a club from playing its best side in such a competition. I would not mind in the slightest if, for example, AC Milan played us with a team consisting of Dutchmen, Germans, Frenchmen, Danes and Swedes. If that had been the team which had won the Italian League, then we would have been quite happy to test ourselves against them. As a result of what happened, I know Alex Ferguson has come to realise that, while we have a big squad of quality players, not enough of them are English if we want to compete in Europe. Having a first team squad which includes two Irishmen, two Welshmen and a Scot, along with the Dane, the Frenchman and the Russian, does cause problems. However, it gave us the taste for the European Cup and we were determined to get back.

It is always reassuring to bounce straight back from a disappointment like that. The only way to do it is to win a big game, and the fixtures had been kind to us in that respect. Just as we had played Arsenal and Sheffield Wednesday after the Honved ties, and Everton after the first Galatasaray match, so we had a Manchester derby on the Saturday of our return from Turkey. Furthermore, City went 2–0 up by half time. Perhaps there had been some hang-over from Galatasaray, but we were not in a good position. That was when we saw Eric Cantona at his best: he scored twice to bring us back into the match and Roy Keane scored the winner. It was a sensational performance which confirmed that we were still on course at home even if we were out of Europe.

Wimbledon were swept aside 3–1, with Gary Pallister scoring one of our goals. Gary gets a bit of stick from the other lads for not scoring very often, but his defensive qualities are admired by all. From struggling just a little to justify his tag as the costliest player in Britain, he has come on in leaps and bounds to become the top centre half around. For somebody standing at six feet four inches he has incredible, if not obvious, pace, has confidence on the ball, and great balance. He has shown with us, and with England of late, that he is the complete centre half.

Our next match was against Ipswich. They were going well themselves at the time, and they came determined to hold us. 0–0 was not the best game of the season, either for us or the spectators. We found it frustrating trying to break them down, while Ipswich played with their two strikers out wide to counter our attacks. This worked, but made it unlikely that they would score themselves. It was something we found time and time again during the season. We expected it to an extent when we were playing at home, but it was a little disturbing when we went away and found teams playing the same way. If they did not have the initiative to have a go at us on their own pitch, when would they? Nevertheless, we still had an eleven point lead over Blackburn, which was comforting after sixteen matches.

We maintained that lead with three points from our match at Coventry. This looked destined to be another goalless draw: having spent ninety minutes without scoring against Ipswich, perhaps we were getting over-anxious at Highfield Road after another hour without scoring. We had missed chances that had gone begging, but then we had a small touch of good fortune. Coventry defender Peter Atherton cleared out towards the right hand touchline, instead of rolling harmlessly into touch, the ball hit the corner flag. Usually, it would deflect for a throw or a corner, but on this occasion it bounced straight back into play at the feet of Ryan Giggs. A pass to Denis Irwin supporting from the back, a cross whipped into the middle and Eric Cantona's head did the rest. This was a year to the day since his arrival at Old Trafford. Coventry hit the bar in the final minute, the ball bouncing to safety. So, ricochets off the ball of two pieces of woodwork could have been said to make all the difference between 1–0 and 0–1. We do not like to think that anything in our preparation is left to chance, but you cannot plan for situations like that.

That apart, we were playing some superb football and entertaining the vast crowds turning out to watch us wherever we went. There were millions seeing us via television as well, for it seemed that we were on at least once a week, often twice. If we had any weaknesses, there was no possibility of hiding them. Everybody, from Alan Hansen to Jimmy Hill, took the opportunity to analyse every aspect of our play from several angles, and at both normal speed and in slow motion. It gave us great pleasure that everyone was so complimentary about our style.

We played with similar skill to beat Everton 2–0 in the Coca Cola Cup at Goodison Park, Peter Schmeichel saving a penalty along the way, before we entered what looked like a difficult December. Norwich were at the top of their game, holding us to a 2–2 draw at Old Trafford. We came up against another first-class young striker that day in Chris Sutton. There are a few around, and he must be rated among the best of them on the evidence of what we saw. A 3–0 win at Sheffield United had us back on winning form, and then we travelled again to Newcastle. I always get a lift from meeting my home-town club, and I am delighted to see Kevin Keegan getting Newcastle back to competing with the best. To think that they were a couple of games away from going into the Third Division shows what a fine job has been done there. As a Newcastle supporter at heart, I am delighted to see it.

We turned in a great performance to see off Aston Villa 3–1 at home, drew with the team emerging as the major threat, Blackburn – thanks to a last minute goal from Paul Ince – and beat poor Oldham 5–2 at Boundary Park. December had been safely negotiated. January was to prove as equally important, with eight matches in three competitions. Leeds came with Chris Fairclough shadowing Eric Cantona wherever he went. Eric was surprised not to find him in the shower next to him after the game.

It was 0–0, during which I suffered a cut from a flying elbow. Brian Deane was the 'culprit', but it was not intentional in any way. The newspapers at the time were sensitive to any incident involving an elbow following what had happened to Gary Mabbutt, but this one was a pure accident.

As professionals we have to be aware that illegal use of the elbow can cause serious injury. You only have to watch a high jumper to know that the arms are used to gain extra lift on take-off. Similarly, when anybody jumps for a ball, he uses his arms. There is a difference between that and jumping in while leading with the elbow. That is pretty rare, and so it should be. Over the top tackles come into the same category, and as professionals we know when such tackles have been committed deliberately. Like the elbow incidents, it is up to responsible players to see that they have no part in our game.

If the Leeds match lacked spectacle, the one which followed offered more than compensation. We went into the Liverpool game with our tails really up. So much passion is involved in these encounters, but it is satisfying for us that the roles have been reversed in recent years with Liverpool trying to topple us rather than the other way around. There is no better place to score than Anfield, and I managed it within the first ten minutes. With goals from Ryan Giggs and Denis Irwin, we were 3–0 up by the interval. A quiet individual, Denis is not one of our players who captures the headlines day in, day out, but he is a proven international and must be one of the best full backs in the business. I can pay him no higher praise than to say that I have never seen anyone give him the run around. He is a good competitor and as brave as they come and, furthermore, the way he strikes a ball is perfection. This one bent as it flew in. But while we harboured thoughts that this could be the night when we gave them a real thrashing, they came storming back to knock us out of our serene stride. They got back to make it 3–3 in a match which, I believe, Liverpool released on video as their game of the season.

From our point of view, it only served to show how we had developed in recent years. We had gone to Anfield, achieved a draw in a highly entertaining game, yet we left disappointed. We strive for perfection, and to throw away a three-goal lead, just as we had a two goal lead against Galatasaray, leaves us feeling thoroughly depressed. We were not totally satisfied with the way we beat Sheffield United in our next match, either. They had knocked us out of the FA Cup the previous season, and here we were travelling to Bramall Lane once more in the Third Round. It was a dour game, brightened by a Mark Hughes goal that came at the end of a dazzling move. Having scored what proved to be the winner, he was sent off for what can only be described as a reckless moment. It will surprise some when I say that this sort of thing was out of character, because he is a quiet, almost shy person off the field. All his emotions come out in his play.

What was in character was the goal Hughes scored. I cannot remember the number of times he has scored the important goal in really big matches. He is one of those players who reacts favourably to the magnitude of a situation and, what is more, they tend to be great goals. Some renowned goalscorers make their reputations from being in the right place to tap in close-range efforts. That is a valuable gift in itself, which makes Mark Hughes priceless for the way in which he bangs them in from all over the place. This season coincided with his benefit year, so at one function he showed a video collection featuring some of the outstanding goals he has scored. It went on for about twenty-five minutes because there were so many. Now he gets teased after every goal he scores that the video will have to be put on a longer tape. Perhaps I can borrow a few when my turn comes; an endless stream of headers does not have quite the same entertainment value!

Mark Hughes is the strongest and the bravest of players, but he does have his flashpoint, although there is never any danger that anyone will be seriously hurt. The incident at Bramall Lane was typical, when he just kicked his opponent up the backside. He probably does not even know himself why he did it. I do not condone such behaviour, but I know that it is just a part of his make-up. If there is one man I would want on my side when we are up against it, Mark Hughes is that man. As a defender, it is comforting to know that he is there when I get the ball. With teams trying to defend so tightly against us, it is important to give the early ball forward when one of their attacks breaks down. This is when Mark comes into his own. I know that I can hit a long pass to him and, providing it is delivered within range, he is good enough to control it and use it. I stress that it is a long pass delivered to a man, and not just a long ball thumped with hope. That will never be the Manchester United way.

Three days later we met Portsmouth in the Fifth Round of the Coca Cola Cup. If we have been vulnerable in defence, it has tended to be when faced with fast, nippy little forwards. Portsmouth had one in Paul Walsh who gave us something of a fright by scoring twice in a 2–2 draw. We went down to Fratton Park for the replay on a quite dreadful night to win 1–0, thanks to a Brian McClair goal. He had a good record in the competition with four goals from seven matches, in one of which he was only a substitute. It is unfortunate that such a gifted player who has played an important part in our success cannot get a permanent place in the team. When he does get in, he always takes his chances. He is the clever one in the side, with academic qualifications to match his footballing prowess. He also has a very quick, dry sense of humour which is often far too intelligent for me, and it is not surprising that he is always the one to run our players' pool and is our representative on the PFA.

In between the Portsmouth matches, we had two 1–0 wins in the League, against Tottenham and Everton. The Everton match was a special one because it came straight after the sad announcement that Sir Matt Busby had died. Sir Matt was more than just the Club President: somehow he represented the whole spirit of Manchester United, and he was responsible for establishing so much that is associated with the Club. He had time for everybody, and even in later life was a fascinating companion to talk to about football. Our thoughts went back to the scenes when we had won the title a few months earlier. He was a focal point of the celebrations and had got immense enjoyment from seeing us bring the title back to Old Trafford. A lovely, kind, generous man, we were all moved by his passing.

There was an eerie atmosphere at the Everton match which was something I have never experienced before. The teams were led on to the field by a lone piper, in recognition of Sir Matt's Scottish background, and the minute's silence was impeccably observed by all. The Everton fans deserve great credit for that. Their behaviour was appreciated by everyone. In fact, there had been a hush all round the ground as we came out, even before the official silence. We were determined to win as a memorial to Sir Matt, but whatever the result, it would not have eased the sadness that was felt around Old Trafford and throughout the football world. We did win, and put on a display worthy of his memory.

It was about this time that people began to think that we had a chance of achieving a treble of the Premiership title, the FA Cup and the Coca Cola Cup. We had opened up a sixteen point gap over Blackburn, even if they did have three games in hand at the time. We beat Norwich 2–0 away in our next match to move into the Fifth Round of the FA Cup, and had already secured a semi-final place in the Coca Cola Cup. Bookmakers had stopped taking bets on us retaining our League title, while only offering something like 11 to 2 against us completing a treble never before achieved and seldom even considered. Alex Ferguson tried to play down the idea in public by saying that in the League it was the best team that came to the top because luck would even itself out. There has to be an element of luck in the cups, and he did not believe we could expect all the luck to be running in our favour throughout the two competitions. Even so, we knew that we were playing well enough to stand a chance.

In the next few weeks we had two visits to London in the League, beating Queens Park Rangers 3–2 and drawing 2–2 with West Ham. We beat Sheffield Wednesday 1–0 at home and 4–1 away over the two legs of the Coca Cola Cup semi-final, and we overcame a potentially tricky tie at Wimbledon with an ease reflected in a 3–0 scoreline in the

Fifth Round of the FA Cup. That run meant we had remained undefeated in an incredible sequence of thirty-four matches. Our only defeat in the League all season had come at the hands of Chelsea, back on September 11th. On March 5th, they were our next opponents at Old Trafford.

There was never any feeling of apprehension about facing Chelsea simply because they had been the only team to beat us in the League: when we were going as well as we were, we could not imagine defeat. We had to accept it, however, when history repeated itself. Just as Gavin Peacock had scored the only goal of the game at Stamford Bridge, so he did at Old Trafford. The season could have taken a drastic turn for the worse the following week when Charlton were our visitors at Old Trafford. That was when resilience and teamwork counted for so much. We were being held by a Charlton side that had beaten Blackburn in the previous round, and they were doing a good containing job on us for most of the first half. That was when Peter Schmeichel came charging out of goal in an attempt to stop one of their breakaways. It was a bit rash, to say the least, but there was no way he intentionally handled. However, their player was through, Peter spread himself and the ball hit his hand while he was outside the area. The ball had been goalbound so, even though he had turned his head, in the circumstances it went down as a hand ball in a certain goal scoring situation. We could have no real grounds for complaint when he was sent off because, even if the ball had not had hit his hand, he might have gone for dangerous play. Referees tend to not take kindly to six-feet-four-inch goalkeepers launching themselves at forwards outside the penalty area.

This meant a reorganisation, with Paul Parker coming off so that Les Sealey could go in goal. It was a case of rolling up the sleeves and calling for an extra effort. The manager's words about luck in the Cup were echoing around Old Trafford, but two goals from Andrei Kanchelskis and another from Mark Hughes saw us through 3–1. The way the fixtures worked out, however, meant that Peter

Schmeichel would be missing from the Coca Cola Cup Final. This was a great shame, for the big Dane is a very popular member of the Manchester United set-up. We all regard him as being of the very highest calibre of goalkeeper, as well as being an important character around the place. He has his moments of eccentricity, like moving up to the opposition penalty area when there is a corner and we are losing in the closing minutes. He did it against Blackburn in our first League meeting and might have caused enough of a diversion for Gary Pallister to head on for Paul Ince to score. He did it again a few weeks later at Wimbledon and actually got his head to the ball. Unfortunately, on that occasion I was just behind him, ready for a free header which I was pretty confident of scoring with, until he intervened and sent the chance wide.

There was no need for such antics in the League match following that Cup victory. Sheffield Wednesday, being a good footballing side, did not confine their ambitions to mere survival. They tried to match our football, but suffered a 5–0 defeat. It was a moment to savour, because things became a little tense after that. There was always going to be the situation where everybody wanted to see us beaten – that is understandable when one club is having everything its own way. It is also understandable that, with what was to happen in the next few weeks, we began to feel that the whole world and all the fates had turned against us.

We went to Swindon who were desperately trying to stay in the top division by playing their adventurous, if naïve, brand of attacking football. The match ended 2–2, but, more significantly, Eric Cantona got himself sent off for stamping on John Moncur after a mid-field clash. It was a stupid thing to do and, again, we could not dispute the decision. We did complain when we played Arsenal at Highbury later that week, however. Again the result was 2–2 and again Eric Cantona was sent off. He was becoming a marked man who could not afford to step out of line in any way. The irony is that he was sent off for actually trying to avoid trouble. Going for a fifty-fifty ball with Nigel Winterburn, Eric attempted to jump out of the way at the last moment. The Arsenal player carried on with his challenge, only for the referee to judge that Eric had jumped at the defender.

I am not one of those people in football who claims that my club and its players are always in the right. It was said that Manchester United were a club of whingers – 'Moanchester United' was one lurid headline. I do believe, however, that if it was justified for Eric Cantona to receive his marching orders at Swindon, it was an error for him to be sent off at Highbury. I can understand how it happened: Eric had perhaps been fortunate to get away with a bad tackle and a stupid back flick at Jeremy Goss during the Cup tie at Norwich, and he had just been seen to be out of order at Swindon. The knives were out, so as soon as he was involved in anything untoward at Highbury, the odds were stacked against him. There have been plenty of cases when video evidence has been used to condemn players, even if the referee missed the incident at the time. I am not against that, but I feel that if the video shows a mistake has been made in the other direction, all concerned should admit they made an error and amend the disciplinary action accordingly. Even a brief look at the video evidence in this case proved without doubt that the referee had been in the wrong.

I am not a great believer in allowing too much legal action in football, but I just wonder if the authorities are over sensitive to such possibilities. Had they agreed that a mistake had been made, would the Club have asked for the match to be replayed with Eric available for the full ninety minutes? Could Eric himself have brought a case against the referee for defamation of character? All a little fanciful perhaps, but it could be that such considerations play a part in the fact that you never hear a referee admitting that he has made a mistake.

As it was, we were deprived of the services of a vital member of our side for five matches. The Swindon sending off naturally would have seen Eric suspended for some of those matches; the absence resulting from the Arsenal incident could conceivably have cost us the League and a place in the Cup Final. Eric Cantona has proved to be such a terrific player that he is virtually impossible to replace. On occasions he has been known to display a dubious temperament, but this is all part of the character of someone I regard as a fantastic player. I only hope that he is remembered for his contributions as a footballer during the 1993–94 season, and not for a couple of silly incidents. I was delighted when he was chosen as the PFA Player of the Year, and only wish he could have done a double by capturing the votes of the Football Writers to recieve the Footballer of the Year award as well. That went to Alan Shearer, with Peter Beardsley second and Eric only third. I was genuinely flattered to be named in fourth place in that poll. Despite all the honours which have come my way in the game, it gave me a thrill to be mentioned among that sort of company.

Eric Cantona had two more games to play before beginning his five match suspension. The first of them was the Coca Cola Cup Final against Aston Villa at Wembley. We were pleased that we had been playing good football throughout, even at this stage of the season. To be honest, we thought we were playing well at Wembley against Ron Atkinson's Villa, despite the fact that he strung a defensive barrier across midfield. I believe I am right in saying that Les Sealey, deputising in goal for the suspended Peter Schmeichel, had only touched the ball once with his hands before Villa took the lead.

We still thought we were in control and would get back on to level terms before going on to win, right up until Villa scored their second goal. That was when the manager decided to play with just three at the back and bring Brian McClair on. Looking back, of course it made sense, but that was not how I felt at the time when I saw the number four card being held up, meaning that I was the one to come off. It was a weird experience, starting the match as captain but then watching it all going on and not really feeling as part of it. It was brought home to me when Mark Hughes had a goal-bound shot turned round by a quite marvellous save from Mark Bosnich. Then Mark Hughes did get one near the end and we still had a chance before the penalty that killed us and our treble hopes for good. Andrei Kanchelskis was back in front of our goal as the ball hit the bar and was driven back in towards goal. The ball struck Andrei on the arm and it had to be a penalty. Unfortunately, the law deems that a player preventing a goal with his hand should receive a red card, so poor Andrei was sent off.

I spoke to the referee about the incident after the match, asking why he could not have just given the penalty without the sending off. He explained that if he had not produced the red card, he would have been in trouble with the authorities who control him. It was all very unfortunate. Another key player was going to be missing, in this case for just one match, but it was the FA Cup semi-final. It also meant that we no longer had hopes of the treble. We had to accept the result, and perhaps Villa just about shaded it overall. Nevertheless, it sunk in afterwards just how close we had come to landing the first leg of what would have been a unique achievement. People say that the worst thing in football is losing a semi-final. Touch wood, I have not experienced that yet at any level during my career, but I cannot believe it can be worse than being on the losing side in a Wembley final. The losers' dressing-room on a final day is a desolate place to be.

Once again, the fixtures decreed that we had a big game coming up to get over the disappointment of the final. Liverpool were waiting to come to Old Trafford on the Wednesday evening. Wembley is a strange place to play: it is a lovely surface but it is slow and tiring. I always feel that it needs to be damp to be at its best, then the ball will fizz over the immaculate grass which can otherwise make it a bit pedestrian at times. This is perhaps why we do not see as many outstanding matches at Wembley as we should: if the ball is not travelling over the surface as well, the players tend to do more running, and it is not just the legs which feel the effort, but the whole body also takes times to grow accustomed to the conditions. We had no time, and it says plenty about our character that we lifted ourselves to beat Liverpool 1-0.

All this time, Blackburn had been narrowing the huge lead we had once enjoyed in the League. They had won their games in hand and, all credit to them, they had put together the sort of run that would have given them the title had it not been for our own results. They had one little stumble when they lost to Wimbledon, but we went into this vital match with a six point lead. We were without Eric Cantona, who was serving his first match under suspension, but nevertheless we went in at half time all square. That suited us, for we knew the onus was on them to win. A draw would have maintained our six point lead and taken us one game closer to the title. Straight from the restart, however, Alan Shearer scored. He had a wonderful season, coming back after a really bad injury, and then scored another as Blackburn went on to win 2–0.

The lead was down to three points and the title was no longer the foregone conclusion it had apparently been when we held a sixteen point lead. Without wishing to appear condescending, Blackburn had made a fantastic effort and deserve all praise for chasing us right up to the line. It is not just with hindsight, however, that I always felt we were in command. We could not afford any slips with Blackburn so close behind us, but we always had points, games or even goal differences in our favour. If that confidence was not necessarily justified, it played a significant part in our success: we believed we would retain the title. Our belief was underlined when we beat Oldham 3-2 in the first of three consecutive matches against our near neighbours. It was a close match, with Oldham needing the points as much as we did, but for a totally different reason. They were in the relegation zone and came close to getting the point they so badly needed. Dion Dublin came off the substitute's bench for the third time in a League match during the season to score his first, vital goal. Another first in this match was a change to the back four. Paul Parker was dropped to accommodate Brian McClair in the starting line-up.

He was back for the second match in our three game series, the semi-final at Wembley. Much of Oldham's attacking strength was based on Rick Holden going down the left of their attack, so it made sense to bring back Paul, for there is no one better at doing a man-to-man marking job. His speed, together with his strength, means that he is ideally suited to such a role, and it was good to have the little man back with us in the thick of it – not that he was there for the whole of that semi-final. A goal down and heading towards the final whistle, we were up against it. Paul Parker was replaced by young Nicky Butt who had been scoring well in the reserves. It was asking a lot of the youngster but something had to be done. Oldham were just forty seconds away from their first ever FA Cup Final while we were forty seconds away from having our season shattered.

If ever there was a moment for Mark Hughes to add to the best of to his video collection, this had to be it. I cannot imagine anyone else in the world getting a goal like the one he conjured up then. It had to be the last chance as the ball was flicked on and he powered in to get a boot to it. He was almost horizontal when he made contact, so how he managed to defy the laws of physics by keeping the ball down was beyond belief. Nevertheless, a perfect volley screamed past the Oldham goalkeeper and nestled into the corner of the net. The relief was so great that it was as if we had won the Cup itself, and not just been given another chance in the semi-final: the fantastic goal from Mark Hughes had been a turning point in the season. The Aston Villa match at Wembley could have been the time when those who had taken the 50 to 1 bet that we would win nothing began to rub their hands – if we had lost at Wembley again in the semi-final, they could have cashed in. It would have been virtually impossible to lift ourselves again. Now it had all changed. We knew that Oldham had just had their chance to beat us. In our mood after that goal, they were not going to get another opportunity.

So it proved in the replay at Maine Road. That was the night when Andrei Kanchelskis put on a virtuoso performance. It was one of the best individual displays I have ever seen on a football field. He was unstoppable. He scored one goal himself in our 4–1 in, and every time he got the ball wide on the right, he was off, moving at blistering pace with the ball under close control the whole time. He has always been popular with the fans, but after this match he was, quite rightly, idolised. There had been talk that he might move back to the Continent because of the lack of regular first team opportunities, but after the incredible display against Oldham, everyone was making all possible efforts to get him to stay. That is good, because this quiet, unassuming lad from the Ukraine has worked really hard at settling into a strange environment. Now he has come to terms with the language and culture, and the way we play. Even so, he sometimes refers to English teams playing volleyball with their feet, rather than playing football.

Our next opponents have often been accused of playing that way, and have achieved incredible results in doing so. We went to Wimbledon knowing that Blackburn had won a League match in midweek and were now level on points, although we had a game in hand. They had played earlier in the day at The Dell against Southampton. Had they got even one point they would have moved us off the top of the League for the first time since the season's tables were published. Against all the odds, Blackburn lost. We then had to go out for our match at Wimbledon knowing that a win would restore a three point lead and we would still have a game in hand. We lost 1–0. Perhaps we were too relaxed after hearing the Blackburn score from earlier in the day but, on the other hand, it might have just been one of those days. All credit to Wimbledon, who just sat off us and allowed us to have the ball and defend deep.

It was not their usual style, but it worked on the day. John Fashanu got a goal and they hung on to that lead. I can never remember playing against Wimbledon when our goalkeeper had nothing to do – nothing, that is, apart from coming up to rob me of what I would like to think was a certain equaliser in the last minute!

The significant thing about the Wimbledon game was that it was the last that Eric Cantona missed for suspension. He came back for our game at home to Manchester City. He had been out for three League and two Cup matches. We had won two, drawn one and lost two. This had not been our usual form, and it was no coincidence that on his return he scored twice in the 2–0 defeat of City. We were back on target for the Premiership title. This was confirmed when we went to Leeds the following Wednesday evening and came away with another 2–0 victory. Andrei Kanchelskis was flying again, adding to a goal by Byan Giggs.

Suddenly it was downhill all the way home. While there were still three matches to go, we could start going into detail. Blackburn could reach 89 points; we had 85 with a game in hand and a superior goal difference. We played on the Sunday at Portman Road where Ipswich were in poor form. When we had played them in November, they were right up with the leaders; now they had slid down the table to such an extent that they were many pundits' favourites for the drop. They went a goal up in twenty minutes before Eric Cantona equalised, and then Ryan Giggs gave us the winner twenty minutes from the end. 88 points in the bag. Over to Blackburn for their match at Highfield Road against Coventry on the Monday evening.

Twelve months earlier we had won the title without playing. A Nick Henry goal for Oldham against Aston Villa had ended Villa's title hopes, and we had celebrated on a grand scale. This time I was at home, watching on Sky as the toasts were made to Julian Darby who had scored twice for Coventry in the win which gave us the title. Blackburn could now only muster 86 points and we had 88 already. Perhaps there was not quite the same degree of euphoria as the year before, because by now we were becoming familiar with celebrating the championship. Seriously, this time round it had been twelve months since we had last won it, as opposed to twenty-three years, so it was understandable if there was not quite the same degree of excitement. There was also the fact that this time the season was not over. We still had the Cup Final to come.

It was still some party, and it was a festive atmosphere at Old Trafford on the Wednesday evening when we beat Southampton 2–0, although I was rested from the game. I was back for the final League match of the season when we only managed a draw with Coventry at Old Trafford. It was an emotional occasion for a number of reasons: the long League season had reached a successful climax, and it also saw the end of Bryan Robson's career as a player with Manchester United. A few weeks earlier he had relinquished the captaincy, so I now had the honour of leading the side even when he was in the team. However, for his last League match in the famous red shirt, I happily handed him back the captain's armband. And, just like twelve months earlier, I was proud to share the honour of collecting the championship trophy with a man who I have greatly admired during my time at Old Trafford. Champions again! Now for our third visit to Wembley in under two months.

The League Cup Final is a fine occasion to be part of, especially when you win. The FA Cup Final is the 'real thing', if I can borrow the advertising slogan of the current sponsors of the League Cup. When the FA Cup Final offers the opportunity of doing the elusive double, then it takes on a whole new dimension. The planning, the anticipation and the excitement all become a little more intense. In mentioning the planning, tribute has to be paid to Alex Ferguson, of course. His was a triumph which put him up with the legendary managers in the game. His name would now go with those of Shankly, Chapman, Nicholson, Ramsey and, yes, Busby. Naturally, success like ours is never down to one man, and the Boss would be the first to pay tribute to the help he has enjoyed from the first team coach, Brian Kidd.

It was leading up to another cup final, the European Cup-winners' Cup Final of 1991, that our popular and highly successful coach, Archie Knox, left the Club. It came as a bit of a jolt when he announced his departure because everyone liked his enthusiastic personality. Training was never ever dull and he was well respected by all the players. Unfortunately, he left for Glasgow Rangers where he has had unbelievable success. Originally at Aberdeen with Alex Ferguson, he moved on to manage Dundee himself before returning to Aberdeen. He had been with Alex Ferguson for a long time, so it was a big decision for him to make. However, going back to Scotland was probably the key factor in making up his mind. The timing was unfortunate for us, but the manager pulled one of his master strokes by appointing Brian Kidd to replace him.

Brian was a good friend of Archie's anyway, having worked on the coaching staff at Old Trafford with responsibility for the juniors. He is another who radiates a good personality and is a genuinely nice fellow who will not hear a bad word spoken about anybody. He has taken on Archie Knox's mantle and has gained the utmost respect from everybody. Furthermore, he must now be the most successful number two there has ever been. He takes training every day and is still as fit as a fiddle himself. In fact, we joke that he hung up his boots too early because he looks as if he has not put on a pound of weight since his playing days, and he also retained his huge appetite for the game. To complete the coaching staff, Bryan 'Pop' Robson took over from Brian Kidd looking after the juniors; Eric Harrison runs the A team, while the reserve team coach is Jim Ryan who was in charge himself at Luton for a time and who was one of the Busby Babes more years ago than he cares to remember. That has got to be as good a team as any club can boast.

It is also the ideal team to prepare our club for the FA Cup Final, with all the special demands that such an occasion puts on everyone. The whole staff of any club looks forward to the big day out, and Manchester United is no exception. The only problem is the demand for tickets, which is quite phenomenal. It is not only the fans looking for tickets that takes the time, the press and other sections of the media also make demands on the players' time because, however much other games are billed as being important, the FA Cup Final is unique. It is an occasion that stands out above all others.

There was a fairly relaxed atmosphere in the Manchester United camp before Wembley 1994. We could relax merely because we had got there and the build-up was all part of the occasion. Most of us had experienced it before, and even those who had not knew what to expect, having seen it all on television in previous years. We were kitted out in our Cup Final suits and went down to Windsor on the Thursday to spend the last few days away from the tension and confusion which precedes the big day. I was surprised how everyone was in such a good frame of mind. I do not think it was necessarily because we had already won the League. It was more a case of quiet determination. Here we were on the verge of making history, with the double there for the taking. Adding to our determination was the fact that Chelsea had beaten us twice in the League. Now we had the opportunity to show that we were the better side despite those results. We were convinced we could take that chance in the one which really mattered.

We were keyed up and eager, but not tense. I have noticed before with this team that we thrive on the big occasion. It might not always show in our play, but this is due to other factors, rather than the mood during preparation. There was a confident buzz in the air with the big game coming up and again, all credit to the management for pitching the level just right. We could have relaxed too much, or we could have become so tense that we could not do ourselves justice. Either way, and the result might have been entirely different.

Having had a training session and press conference in

Manchester before leaving the hotel where we were staying, the Oakley Court in Windsor, helped create the right
atmosphere of relaxation. So did excursions like a boat trip
along the Thames on the Friday before the game. We also
went along to Bisham Abbey for a spot of light training
and it was there that I mentioned to Eric Cantona that we
would be awarded a penalty in the Final. What made me
say it, I do not know, for we had been awarded only two
during the entire season until that point. He shrugged his
shoulders, threw his arms out wide and said 'Penalty, no
problem; I'll score'.

Eric was going to have a bit of penalty practice, but decided
against it as there were a few cameras about and he did not
want Dmitiri Kharine, Chelsea's Russian goalkeeper, to learn
from the morning papers or see on television which way he
intended putting a spot kick. Even without the practice, he
assured me he would score. He was not being boastful; he
just had total belief in himself. I was interested to see how
confident he was, because for three and a half years I had
been the regular penalty taker. Quite when I was deposed I
am not sure, but nobody could have been better suited to
the task than Eric Cantona.

The feeling of excitement increased towards the game
itself but, again, it was always controlled excitement. We
were delighted to see the rain begin, because we knew it
would make the surface more to our liking. Even so, we
really did not play as we should have done in the first half.
Any member of the side who thought we had was quickly
put right by the manager at half time. All credit to Chelsea
for making life so difficult for us. They must have been
thinking that things were not going to go their way when
they saw Gavin Peacock's clever lob bounce back off the
cross bar during the first half, just as we knew we had got
away with it.

We started to play better after half time, and once we had
got the first penalty, we really believed we were unstoppable.
I must admit that I turned away as Eric Cantona took that

vital kick. I usually do if I am not taking them myself. I watched Peter Schmeichel until his reaction and the crowd's told me that we were one up and on our way. In retrospect, it was incredible how Eric Cantona maintained his self-belief right up to the moment he stroked the ball in. He looked as if he was taking the practice kick he had decided against the day before. Having looked away for the first penalty, superstitious as footballers are, there was no way I would look at the second one which Eric put in exactly the same place. He was quoted afterwards as saying that he was not nervous: 'It is just a game, not a war. If you are nervous in this sort of game, it is better to stop playing.' What a way to look at it! I am not sure I would have had exactly the same attitude, but I must admit that I would not have minded taking them. If Eric had not been on the pitch, it would have been down to me and I rather think I would have enjoyed the opportunity. Having said that, it is when you are the penalty taker in a Cup Final that nerves of steel are required, because the eyes of the whole world are focused on you.

The first goal was the important one. Once we had got in front, Chelsea were forced to come at us and, as a result, left the gaps which we had the pace and skill to exploit. They had to abandon the tactic of trying to stifle us, and for fifteen to twenty minutes, Chelsea became just a little reckless in the way they pressed forward. There was controversy about the award of the second penalty. It was one of those borderline decisions and, if I had been playing for Chelsea, I would have been annoyed, but these things tend to even themselves out over the course of time. I had felt aggrieved at being booked earlier for what I thought had been a fair challenge on a slippery surface. To be honest, I believe that it was the first goal which so so important, and there could have been no doubt about that decision.

Once that one had gone in, it became evident that we were going to win. Mark Hughes seized on a mistake in the Chelsea defence to get the third before Paul Ince went on a penetrating run to set up Brian McClair for the fourth in injury time. It was unselfish of Paul and good that Brian, on as a substitute, should get his name on the scoresheet. It says something for Alex Ferguson's management that he was prepared to be totally objective about his choice of substitutes for the match. Lee Sharpe and Brian McClair were chosen as the outfield players because he felt they presented him with most options. Sadly, this also meant that there was no place for Bryan Robson. It would have been good to see Robbo involved in such a big game at the end of his United career, but the heart could not be allowed to rule the head. He was left as an onlooker, wearing his suit rather than the red shirt he had worn so often on such occasions.

When the final whistle was blown, the celebrations began and continued for hours. After that marvellous moment when I received the Cup from the Duchess of Kent, there were the photographs, the interviews and the lap of honour. When we eventually left Wembley we had a private dinner for the players, wives and close friends, arranged at the Metropole. It would have been memorable had any of us been able to remember what happened! We certainly let our hair down and, as captain, I felt it was my duty to supervise the celebrations. That meant I was the last to leave the event at approximately 5.30 on the Sunday morning.

Then it was back to Manchester for the now traditional ride through the city on an open top bus. As on previous occasions, thousands upon thousands of people lined the route and cheered us all the way. If such triumphal processions need any novelty, this time there were both the Premiership trophy and the FA Cup to be shown to the throng. The enormity of what we had achieved began to sink in, especially when an interviewer informed me that I was the first Englishman to captain a double-winning team. Danny Blanchflower was an Irishman, while Frank McLintock and Alan Hansen were both Scots. Here was I, captain of a team which I believed deserved to be included in the company of Spurs, Arsenal and Liverpool. We had played thirty-four matches and lost only four. We had won the Premiership and the FA Cup; we had the Charity Shield in our possession, while the reserve team had won their Pontins League as well. 1993–94 was quite a season for Manchester United and Steve Bruce.

Chapter Two

The major part of my professional career has been spent in one of the great footballing areas of England – Manchester. I was born and brought up in another – Newcastle. In fact, I was born just outside Newcastle in a village called Corbridge on New Year's Eve in 1960. The Bruce family did not live there, but at that time of year my mother was pleased to be admitted to any hospital that would take her. Sheenagh, my mother, who comes from Bangor in Northern Ireland met my father, Joe, when she was over in the Newcastle area and he was doing his national service in the army. He became a fitter/turner with a local engineering company and played amateur football for fun. His contemporaries tell me that he possessed all the skills and could play but, as he himself admits, he was lazy and never made the most of his footballing abilities.

He was, however, a keen Newcastle United supporter and made sure that I was brought up in a black and white household. So, too, was my younger brother, Ian, but he has never really taken to the game. Like most boys in the area he still shows an interest in Newcastle and he will come to watch me. My father has always watched me play, as has my mother. Between them they must have travelled to every school and junior-club ground in the North East to see me play football. This encouragement is important for someone who is developing a passion for the game, and my father always ensured that I had a decent football with which to play. I was also lucky in that our house in Daisy Hill, near the shipyards in Wallsend, backed on to a playing field so I only had to hop over the back fence to have a kick around. It might have been a fairly tough area, but even at that early age I was always involved in football.

I remember spending every waking moment being involved with the game. I was lucky in that I did not quite experience the classic childhood of a footballer that consists of playing with a bundle of tied-up rags for a ball and chalking goalposts on the wall. I had a decent ball and grass to play on. We would, however, lay down jackets for goalposts and every day after school my mates and I would play until we were called in for tea or it became dark, and sometimes even after dark. I was only happy when kicking a ball about.

As well as playing I was also taken to St James's Park on occasions to watch Newcastle United. I can hardly remember the early matches I saw because I was so young, but players like that classy wing-half, Jim Iley, are still clear in my mind. He had left Newcastle when, as a nine-year-old, I enjoyed watching what was at that time the biggest game of my life. I had seen some of the early matches played by Newcastle in the European Fairs Cup as it was known before becoming the UEFA Cup. Then one evening my father woke me up in bed to tell me that he had managed to get hold of a couple of tickets for the first leg of the final itself, against Ujpest Dozsa. Before going away for the second leg which they won 3–2, Newcastle beat the Hungarians at St James's Park 3–0. The ground was absolutely packed and I was passed over the heads of the crowd so that I could get a place near the front. I thought the whole atmosphere was just brilliant.

Another vivid memory from my childhood concerned the first time football clashed with something else. I was at Walker Gate Primary School and, as a ten-year-old, I was due to have a trial for the school Under 11 side. That was scheduled to take place at exactly the same time as my parents had decided to take us on holiday. As I was a year younger than most of the other lads the school had made a special concession for me to take part, and there was no way that I wanted to miss it. I stated quite clearly that I was not going on the family holiday; I was going to stay behind to play football. It was only when they found out from the schoolmaster that he regarded me as good enough to get in without the trial that my parents finally persuaded me to go away on the holiday with them.

That schoolmaster was called Michael Bell. He was a big, red-headed man who made quite an impression on me by putting me in the team. Schoolboy football in the North East was absolutely fantastic then as so many people gave up their time to organise it. Even at infant-school level there were well-administered leagues and every team had its own full set of kit. No wonder so many players from the region went on to play professional football. It was in one of the local competitions the following year that I won my first footballing trophy – the Bagnell Cup. I was captain of the team and was still wearing my first-ever pair of boots given to me by my Aunt Frances and Uncle Davy. It was during this competition that my mother took her turn at washing the team kit. Mr Bell sent her a note to thank her and made a prophetic remark: 'Thanks a lot for washing the green strips. I know emerald green is probably your favourite colour, but you shouldn't have gone to so much bother. However, when Stephen's playing for Manchester United I don't think you'll have the bother of washing his strip.' Did he just pluck the name of a big club out of the air or was he some sort of fortune-teller? It was a shame that Walker Gate Primary wore green and white rather than red and white!

During my time at the school I also got into the Newcastle Boys team. I had to go to trials at a place called Montague on the west side of Newcastle, while I came from the east side. That made it quite an expedition, and there was more than one trial. I went from stage to stage before eventually getting into the team, at which point my father bought me my first watch to celebrate. I stayed in that Newcastle Boys side all the way through from Under 11 to Under 16 when I left school. This was my first taste of representative football, and if we were not a very successful side in terms of winning trophies, it was a good side in which to play for the experience it offered. My selection also confirmed that I might just have an outside chance of going on to greater things in the game.

When I was twelve I joined a well-known boys club in the area, Wallsend Boys Club, which proved to be a step that was to have far-reaching consequences. The man who ran it, Pete Kirkley, was to have a big influence on a lot of the things that were to happen to me in my career. He put together a successful team in my year, with the likes of Peter Beardsley who made his name with Newcastle as well as becoming an established England international player, and Rob Hindmarch who became captain of Sunderland. This side won just about everything there was going and remained unbeaten for four or five years.

Pete Kirkley was also the man who was responsible for my first taste of life with a professional football club. He used to do some scouting for Burnley and he took me along to Turf Moor for a trial. In fact, I spent my twelfth birthday in a hotel in Burnley when I was at the Lancashire club for my trial. It had all come about a little earlier when I had returned home one evening from visiting friends and there was a car parked outside our house, from which two men were just emerging. It was about 8.30 p.m. and one of the men, Pete Kirkley, remarked that I should have been home before that time. The other turned out to be Ken Walshaw, who was a North Easterner who had played League football for Lincoln, Carlisle and Bradford City, having started as an apprentice with Sunderland. He was then the area scout for Burnley. He had watched me play the previous weekend and had come to tell my parents that he would like me to go for a trial.

For a lad who by now had decided he wanted to be nothing else other than a professional footballer this was the most fantastic news. I had become more and more engrossed in the game as my involvement with the boys club developed. It might have been a narrow existence but

I was interested in only one thing and that was football. Bearing that in mind, imagine what it meant to me to be offered a chance like this. To be fair, I realise now that I did not do myself justice. I never did anything outstanding but still went along every school holiday to spend time at the club.

This association continued for a couple of years until I reached that crucial period for a schoolboy footballer, around the fourteen-to-fifteen age-group. At this important stage in my embryonic career I was, to put not too fine a point on it, a little weed. Compared with the other strapping lads who were around I was tiny. When I was eleven and twelve I was the big lad, but for the next two years I hardly grew and was overtaken by everyone else. The message from Burnley and everywhere else that I was touted around for schoolboy trials – Newcastle, Sunderland, Derby, Sheffield Wednesday, Bolton – was always the same. I was too small to cope with the physical rigours of professional football even if they did all agree that I might have had something going for me in the skills department. The skills would count for nothing if I was not big enough or strong enough to look after myself in a tough game.

It was terribly frustrating, especially as I was by now old enough to appreciate the situation fully. Despite my determination to prove them all wrong, I began to wonder if they might be right after all. Perhaps I was destined to become one of the army of what could be termed, with all modesty, talented schoolboy footballers who lacked just one quality that would allow them to break through to the highest level. That missing quality might be skill, mental approach, physical capability or even luck. Having been told so often that I was too small I began to believe that I might have a problem with my physical capability, and I knew I was right out of luck. Maybe I should look for another career.

Having said that, I was still playing for the Newcastle Boys team and had been chosen for the Northumberland Under 15 county side, so I felt that I must have had something going for me. In some people's eyes I still had something to offer. Despite all the knock-backs I was determined to keep plugging away so that I could never look back and be forced to admit that I had not given myself every possible chance.

I had changed schools when I was eleven and was now attending the massive Benfield Comprehensive School along with some two thousand other pupils. That might sound a little daunting, but it was a brand new school with marvellous facilities for all types of sport. We had a good school football team that won a few cups, so my weekends were taken up with playing for the school on Saturdays and Wallsend Boys Club on a Sunday. That club became a large part of my life, because I would be there on Tuesday and Thursday evenings for five-a-side football and on Wednesdays for training.

Apart from being around the club, I also enjoyed myself at school. Even there my life centred on sport. Football was always the major one for me, but if we did not have a match I would turn out for the rugby team. In the summer I played cricket, which I also loved and went on to play at a goodish standard with Wallsend. In fact, I enjoyed my cricket as much as football and still follow the game, but I felt I did not play it so well and would not be able to advance in it as I hoped to progress in football. I was in the cross-country-running team, the swimming team and the basketball team. I would have a go at anything. It was also at school that I met my wife, Janet. She too was keen on sport and became Newcastle Schools champion as a sprinter.

I always regard myself as being fortunate in attending a school that encouraged sport and had all these sporting facilities. Having said that, facilities are not much use unless there are members of staff to ensure that they are properly utilised. One of our teachers was a man called John Watson who graduated through the local leagues to become a top referee. We had kept in touch for a while after I had left school and I knew that he was making progress, but I did not realise just how far he had gone until I was captain of the

Manchester United team against Wimbledon and the referee was none other than the same John Watson. I met him before the match and then reported back to the rest of the team. 'We'll have no problem with the ref. today, lads. He used to take me at school and he was a good schoolmaster so I'm sure he'll be a good referee.' Imagine the stick I took when he turned down an absolutely blatant penalty! It was right in front of the Stretford End, so he got booed and hissed throughout the rest of the game. My treatment by the rest of the team was not much better, even if it was given in a more light-hearted manner.

All that was in the future when I reached the age of sixteen and was about to take my O levels in English language and English literature out into the big, wide world. That was when Pete Kirkley stepped in again and fixed me up with a job in the Wallsend Sports Centre for the period between the end of my exams and the start of the football season. At the same time he got me another trial with a League club, this time at Southport. It went quite well and I thought I had a chance there. Hugh Fisher, the manager, seemed reasonably impressed with my performances playing the odd match with the A team, and I even travelled with the first team to an away-game at Watford to gain experience. Watford finished in the top half of the Fourth Division that season under their new manager, a certain Graham Taylor, and chairman Elton John. They were on their way up in the football world and beat Southport 2–0 that day. Southport were moving in the opposite direction, and the defeat ensured that they would be applying for re-election at the end of the season.

Hugh Fisher had said to me 'We'll see; we'll see what happens about the re-election' as the players dispersed at the end of the season. Nothing did happen with Southport as far as I was concerned. Having waited to hear that the club had been re-elected to play in the Fourth Division again, the manager said that he had no money available even to consider taking on an apprentice. As things turned out it was perhaps all for the best. I was sitting in the bath a year later when I heard on the radio that, this time, Southport had not been re-elected. I wonder how many of their players managed to find new clubs in the League, and what would have happened to me if I had been taken on and had just begun my career at Haig Avenue when the end came.

That was not the way I saw things in 1977. I needed a proper job if I was not going to be taken on to serve an apprenticeship in football. I could not stay at the sports centre doing odd jobs like setting up the tennis nets. Fortunately for me, my cousin David Armstrong pulled a few strings and got me an interview down at the Swan Hunter shipyard for a job as a trainee plumber. It was not what I wanted to do, but I had little choice. To be honest, I had no choice and I realised that any job was better than no job even if no other job could measure up to my ambition to play professional football.

I was resigned to the fact that I would be going into the shipyard and, furthermore, there was just about to be a significant change in my footballing activities. I had gone right through the teams at the Wallsend Boys Club and was at the end of my last season. The team that had been together for so long was breaking up and we were about to go our separate ways. We had received an invitation to take part in an international youth tournament that was to take place at Charterhouse, a public school in Surrey. To celebrate our successful years together we decided to enter and so set off for the South.

We stayed in a YMCA hostel and felt that we were really there to enjoy ourselves rather than to play serious football. We had been taking it all very seriously for the previous five years and we were now looking to go out in a blaze of fun. In spite of the fact that we were all sixteen and down in London for a bit of a giggle, we did make progress in the competition at the expense of some of the foreign sides who had come over specifically to impress. Perhaps there is room for a more relaxed approach on occasions. Whether that's true or not, unknown to me, Pete Kirkley had arranged for the manager of Gillingham, Gerry Summers, to come and have a look at me. Gerry Summers had been involved in football for a long time, beginning his playing career with West Bromwich Albion when they were a prominent First Division side. He had moved to Sheffield United for six seasons before spells with Hull and Walsall. Now he was running the Kent club and agreed to come along to Charterhouse to watch us in the final of the tournament.

As I was walking off the pitch at the end of the game Pete Kirkley introduced me to him. In spite of the fact that we had lost I had done enough in the game to impress him and he asked whether I would be prepared to go down to Gillingham for a trial. What a dilemma for a football-mad sixteen-year-old who was due to start work in the shipyard in a week's time. I would have loved to have said yes and gone without a second thought, but I had to explain the situation. Gerry Summers considered the position and said that he would contact Swan Hunter and ask them to delay the date on which I was to start. Then, if anything went wrong, I would still have a job to go back to but here was one last chance to get into professional football. I needed no further time to think about it. If I had been completely honest with him I would have asked which division they were in, and even where the town of Gillingham was. I did not have a clue that they were one of the furthest League clubs away from Newcastle, but it did not matter to me at that stage.

I telephoned my parents and told them that I was going to Gillingham for a trial, and they naturally asked all the correct questions that parents should about who had asked me to go and, basically, wanted to know would I be OK. In my innocence and enthusiasm I said that all was well and so it was off to Kent for yet another trial. At the end of that week Gerry Summers was unable to make a decision about me. He said he wanted to have a proper look at me for a month throughout the pre-season training period. Again, I had to explain the situation to the shipyard at a time when jobs were hard to come by. Gerry Summers told me that he had rung my potential employers and they had agreed to keep the job open. Whether he ever did ring I never found out. I did not even try to find out in case Swan Hunter were not really being so understanding, nor did I tell my parents that I had not checked in case it was not true. He said the job was to be held open and that was all I wanted to hear.

When I went back for this crucial month there were a few more triallists on the scene. We were all aware of the competition and there were times when I thought that I might fail to stand out in such company. In case it might be thought that there was no real pressure with a club like Gillingham it should be said that there was another lad from the North East who came down for a trial. He was another member of the Wallsend Boys Club who Pete Kirkley brought to the notice of Gerry Summers. This same lad was also turned down by Cambridge United. His name was Peter Beardsley. However, at the end of the month, Gerry Summers announced that only two of those present were to be offered contracts as apprentice professionals. One was a lad with whom I had become good pals called Colin Ford, who went on to make just one League appearance for Gillingham during which he was substituted. The other was announced as Steve Bruce.

At first I could not believe it. After Newcastle, Sunderland, Derby, Sheffield Wednesday, Bolton and Southport, here at last was a League club prepared to offer me a contract to employ me as a professional footballer. Let alone reading the small print, I ignored the large print as well. It was a contract and it had my name on it. I signed. I felt sorry for the boys who had not been taken on, especially a lad called Peter Hobday who was a good centre-half. He lived locally and Gillingham kept him on so that we played alongside one another in the youth team. Eventually he was offered a contract when he reached nineteen, and he was taken on. Although he never played in the first team, he later went to Germany to play with success in the Bundesliga.

Meanwhile, after I was told the news that I was to be

taken on as an apprentice, Gerry Summers gave me a few days off to go back home to get sorted out. It was then that it all began to sink in. As a suddenly very young and inexperienced sixteen-year-old I was to leave home, my family and all my friends, including Janet, to go and live in digs over three hundred miles away. It seemed even further as I travelled back on the train to begin my new life as an apprentice professional footballer with more than just a hint of apprehension.

Chapter Three

With some justification, the general public tend to regard life in professional football as being on the glamorous side. I assure you that life as an apprentice was far from glamorous. It had been hard to leave home and no easier to settle in to life in the Medway towns, a fairly featureless area of Kent around that point where the River Medway flows into the southern side of the Thames Estuary. There are some scenic places around, and some of the people were very friendly and welcoming but, having said that, it was nothing like home. For one thing, football is everything on Tyneside; it did not seem to be as important to the people living alongside the Medway.

I was being paid the sum of twelve pounds a week with a two-pound bonus if the youth team won, as well as having my digs paid for by the club. Muriel and Sam Legg, with whom I was lodging, did their best to make me feel welcome in their home, but I was still suffering terribly from homesickness. It is a problem that besets many a young lad when, at that age, he suddenly finds himself thrown into a strange environment a long way from home. On one hand, the lack of money did not particularly bother me and I did have a chance, as an apprentice, of making it in the professional game. After all the effort I had made to get into that position it meant a lot to me. On the other hand, had someone suggested in those first few months that I should pack it all in and go home, I probably would have done so. Instead of that, my parents always encouraged me to stick at it and, looking back, it is probably just as well they did not try to entice me back to the North East. I would not have taken much persuading.

To make matters worse, Colin Ford, the other apprentice taken on at the same time, was a local lad and he continued to live at home. He and his family were very good to me, but it is one thing to be welcomed into someone else's home and another to be in your own home. As anyone who has ever been in the same situation will tell you, it is in the low moments that the mind immediately starts to drift to the good times back home. You imagine what will be happening at that particular time of day, and even the most mundane occurrence conjures up a longing to be back in familiar surroundings.

The actual football was fine, and one of the arguments in favour of being at a small club was that I got to play more games than I might have done at one of the big city clubs. Not only did I play for the youth team on a Saturday in the South-east Counties' League, but I also got a chance to play in the reserve side in the Mid-week League. I used to enjoy playing against the likes of Arsenal, Tottenham, Chelsea and Queen's Park Rangers. It gave me an understanding of the difference between the big clubs and us. Gillingham were always the minnows, and it was fun to take on the big boys and, quite often, to beat them.

Nowadays apprentices are given time to further their education outside football which must be a good thing. In my time there was nothing of the sort. I used to have to catch the twenty-past-eight bus in the morning to get in by nine o'clock. The next bus was not until eight forty-five, and that did not arrive until just after nine. It was fortunate that the stop was just outside the digs, so there was little excuse for missing the bus. Before training began, Colin and I were responsible for getting out everybody's kit and towel, and making sure that all the boots were available. Then we went out for training before returning to what might be termed domestic duties. The kit was only washed once a week, even if it was caked in mud, but we had to collect it all in and hang it up around a big old boiler. By the end of the week the smell was absolutely horrendous.

After that came what was probably the hardest job of all. There were about thirty professionals at the club whose boots all needed cleaning. The rest of the training kit might be allowed to fester but boots were thought of as tools of a footballer's trade and so had to be cleaned. I must have spent hours and hours in the little old boot-room at Priestfield Stadium, getting the mud off, generally cleaning and checking all the studs. Even after that we had not finished. We had to clean the floors, clean the bathrooms and wash the showers. I sometimes wondered whether I had become an apprentice to a laundry or a commercial cleaning company rather than to a football club.

I must admit that, despite the chores, I enjoyed being around the club all the time. By the end of my apprenticeship I knew where everything was and certainly had an appreciation of the fact that there is more to being part of a club than kicking a ball on a Saturday afternoon. I had to sweep the terraces and paint the roof if it needed painting. In fact, whatever menial task needed doing, we had to pitch in and help out. On one occasion there was a burst pipe in a small corridor leading down a slight slope into the manager's office. Gerry Summers, who might have been a good manager but was no King Canute, came out screaming and bawling that something had to be done to stem the tide. Colin Ford and I were there, and so we were the ones who had to set to with shovels, buckets, towels and anything else that came to hand to try to stop the water getting down to the office. Despite the fact that water was by now absolutely gushing out, we managed to keep it away from his office and Gerry Summers was so pleased that he gave us a fiver each. Being virtually half a week's wages, we were delighted with our unexpected windfall. It was a pity, in a way, that I had not started that plumber's course at Swan Hunter as I might have got a tenner to myself.

Apart from the chores to be done in an afternoon, we

sometimes got some help with our football from the assistant manager, Alan Hodgkinson. He had reached the top as a player despite the handicap of being a five-foot nine-and-a-half-inch goalkeeper. He had a long and distinguished career at Sheffield United during which he made nearly six hundred appearances for them, and kept goal for England. It was valuable to tap in to the experience of someone like him, and he is someone with whom I have stayed in touch from my days with Gillingham because he now does some coaching with the goalkeepers at Old Trafford. Those extra sessions were a bonus compared with the usual jobs of keeping the place spick and span. Often it would be four or five o'clock before I finished, but I did not mind because, quite honestly, there was not much to go home to anyway.

There were some young professionals around the club that I became friends with, like an Irishman by the name of Pat Walker and George Clark, a Scot. We shared digs at one stage, and often went to the pub round the corner for a drink in the evening. They would not let me go to the bar when we did, not because they felt sorry for me on my low income, but because I still looked so young and was so small that they were afraid that we would all get thrown out if the landlord spotted me. Even by that age I had still not filled out.

Someone else who spotted that I was very young and a long way from home was the youth team manager, Bill Collins. His own playing career had been affected by the war. An Irishman, he had played for Belfast Celtic before moving over first to Luton and then to Gillingham when they had just been re-elected back into the old Division Three (South). He only played in thirteen League matches but stayed with the club. I was thankful he did because he had a significant bearing on my life and career by taking me under his wing. He regularly invited me to his house and, after my seven years with Gillingham, I had become part of the fixtures and fittings.

Whatever problem I had, or if I was just feeling a bit

lonely, I would go round to Bill's house and sit with him and his wife, Betty, and his two daughters, Michelle and Julie, who made up for the family I had left so far away on Tyneside. Bill was very much a father-figure to me. He was one of those people who never capture the headlines and, consequently, is never appreciated the way he should be. Every club needs a Bill Collins, and without someone like him looking after the youngest members of the club staff, so many more would go out of the game or off the rails, or both.

The type of digs can also be crucial to the happiness of a youngster. If Bill Collins treated me like a son, my landlady, Peg Hatton, was like a mother to me. If I was late in I would find a hot-water bottle in my bed and she could not have been kinder to me. People would ask why I did not move into a flat or house of my own at twenty-one or twenty-two, but when I was being looked after as I was, why make life more uncomfortable? She suffered from a serious illness after I left and I was sad that I could not be there to look after her after what she had done for me. Happily she recovered and I still see her every now and then.

I was lucky to have Peg looking after me at home and Bill Collins, or Buster as he was known, to take care of me at the club. He seemed to reserve a special place for me, but he was very good to all the youngsters at the club. There were not too many of them, because our youth team tended to consist of several schoolboys and triallists who had not been signed on any permanent basis. They all had a great respect for Bill Collins, and it was through him that I became great friends with a fellow called Billy Hughes. Billy was the same age as me – sixteen – yet had already played in the first team at Gillingham. Another good friend was Dean White. A couple of years older than Billy and me, he was already a first-team player after serving his apprenticeship with Chelsea. He played over a hundred games for Gillingham before moving to Millwall.

Dean did not stand out as a player in quite the same way

as Billy. I would watch him in training and marvel at his ability. For a sixteen-year-old he was rather special. He was the boy wonder and attracted a lot of media attention. His name was inevitably linked with the big clubs, yet he was one of those precocious talents who does not really 'train on', as they say in horse-racing parlance. At the end of the 1980–81 season, he was given a free transfer by Gillingham. Alan Mullery took him on at Crystal Palace for the 1981–82 season when he played a handful of games before moving on to Wimbledon. After a couple of games there his contract was cancelled and he headed off to South Africa. Happily, the last I heard, he was enjoying himself out there.

In those early days at Gillingham we became close friends. Billy's family came from Folkestone, so I often went down there with him at weekends. He and his family were good to me, and as I was on peanuts while he was in the first team, he usually paid when we went out socially. He was the one who had a car first and could afford to buy the drinks. Over a quiet pint we would confide in each other about our hopes and aspirations in the game. Bearing in mind what Billy had already achieved and what a future apparently stretched out before him, it seems strange that the then struggling apprentice has had virtually all his dreams fulfilled while his, in the main, crumbled to dust. At least he was to be around when I took a major step in my life. He was my best man when Janet and I got married in 1983.

All that was in the future during my first year as an apprentice at Gillingham. In general I enjoyed it, perhaps because I had tried so hard to get a chance that I was determined to make it all worthwhile. At the same time, I found it a bit of a struggle to come to terms with my new way of life. Looking back, there was quite a lot happening all at once. I had left home, left school, started work, moved to an entirely new area, and I was growing up all at the same time. There were changes in my life in football as well, because I had been converted into a central defender. Apart from playing a few games as a striker for the boys club, I had always played in midfield.

It was Bill Collins who played as big a part in seeing that my professional future was progressing along the right lines as he did in ensuring that my domestic life was happy. During this first year at Gillingham he suggested that my game might be suited to playing at the heart of the defence. He said that I was pretty good in the air, considering my size, and that I read the game pretty well. Furthermore, having been the little weed that I mentioned earlier, I had suddenly at the age of fifteen started to shoot up and had really outgrown my strength. I had become tall and gangly and, as I had grown, I seemed to lose my pace. Pace was vital in midfield but was of less importance at the back and so I moved to a position where I could feel more comfortable. I gradually settled there and began to enjoy the extra responsibility that went with the position.

During my first few months I remember wanting Christmas to come round so that I could get back home to the North East for a few days to see everybody. However, I had to put such thoughts to the back of my mind and concentrate on my football. In spite of its size our youth team had a fair season in the South-east Counties League. We finished sixth out of sixteen teams and did better than some of the big clubs like Arsenal, Tottenham, West Ham and Norwich. I felt that facing the challenge of meeting teams representing such clubs was the most satisfying aspect of it all. I suppose I always had a little idea in the back of my mind that if I did well against the top clubs I might be spotted by them, but the greatest sense of satisfaction came just from beating them.

They had the pick of all the youngsters around, and that was certainly not the case with Gillingham who had to make do with what might be termed the left-overs. We seldom had a settled team and could never boast the schoolboy stars. I was coming up against players like Clive Allen, who even at that early stage of his career had a reputation of being a prolific goal-scorer with Queen's Park Rangers. Yet I was finding that centre-half suited me and I was becoming more confident in the position. Compared with all the activity and effort in midfield I found it easier to play at the back. I felt I had achieved a good deal when my first season as an apprentice came to an end.

I went back to Newcastle for the summer and spent eight weeks living at home. It was a time to do virtually nothing apart from relaxing, taking it easy and going round to see my old friends. I must admit that I went round with a little bit of a swagger, enjoying my new status as a real footballer, but I hope it was nothing more than that. It was great to be back among my own folk but, as the summer went by, I began to realise that I was going to be leaving very soon to return to Gillingham virtually to start all over again. This was to be the important season, because at the end of it decisions would be made about who was to be offered terms as a full professional and who was to be allowed to move on. An apprentice released by Arsenal might hope to be offered a contract by a smaller club. With all due respect, anyone released by Gillingham could not go much further down the scale to find a club. With this idea in my thoughts and having to leave home to go into new digs, it made the journey back south seem even longer than before.

As it turned out, the 1978–79 season proved to be a good one. The highlight must be getting called up for the England Youth team. Caps at youth level can often lead on to full international caps. For me, however, my eight youth caps stopped me from playing full international football. That was to come later, but at the time I was absolutely thrilled to have been noticed at such a level. Such recognition did not often come to players from our club, and it was a little daunting to look through the side at the other players and the clubs they represented: John Lukic of Leeds, who went on to win Championship medals with Leeds and Arsenal; Steve Mackenzie, then with Crystal Palace but who later went to Manchester City for over a million pounds; Paul Allen, who played in an FA Cup-winning side for West

Ham; Clive Allen who, as I mentioned earlier, was then with Queen's Park Rangers; another million-pound man, Justin Fashanu of Norwich; Gary Shaw and Brendan Ormsby of Aston Villa. Then there was me, from little Gillingham. I must admit to feeling somewhat inferior to this exalted company, but immensely proud for Gillingham.

The side had played a number of internationals during the first part of the 1978–79 season. At that time one of the central defenders was Rob Hindmarch of Sunderland, with whom I had played in the Wallsend Boys Club team. When the side to play against Belgium in Brussels on 17th January 1979 was announced, he was out and I was in. We won with a score of 4–0 and I was retained in the team the following month when England played Italy in a qualifying tie for the UEFA Youth Tournament which was to take place in May in Austria. The first leg was played in the Olympic Stadium in Rome and, even if there were only a couple of thousand people watching, it was still a wonderful experience. We won 1–0 out there and then 2–0 at Villa Park in the second leg to qualify for Austria.

This was my first taste of what might be termed the big time. To play for my country, at whatever level, was almost unbelievable. I had never expected such an honour and it came close to overwhelming me. I got a terrific feeling from flying out with England, getting an England blazer and being pampered to a degree I had not experienced before. It also meant a lot to me to be appearing alongside players from the top clubs and to realise that I was up there with them at that stage. At least, the manager John Cartwright considered me to be their equal by retaining me in the side for the rest of the season. He operated at Crystal Palace and saw me play against them. He also assured me that I had impressed him on the numerous other occasions he had seen me play. Furthermore, he said that all the talk on the circuit indicated that I was the best centre-half around in that age-group. He might just have been trying to encourage me, but his words certainly made me feel much more confident of my own ability.

The tournament was staged at the end of May. England began the group matches well by beating Czechoslovakia 3–0 and following that with a similar win over Malta, when I managed to get my name on the score-sheet. The last group match was a special one because we were playing against West Germany. Ever since 1966 such encounters, at whatever level they were played, took on an extra dimension. We were well aware of this and were naturally delighted to win 2–0 to secure a place in the semi-finals. There we played Bulgaria and lost 1–0 when Clive Allen hit the post with a penalty in the last minute. Instead of lining up in the final we had to contend with a third and fourth place play-off against France. That ended in a goalless draw, but we won 4–3 on penalties for a creditable third place in the tournament.

After making my international début I came close to making my League début for Gillingham. The club was involved in a promotion race and was striving to get up into the Second Division for the first time ever having always been in the Third and Fourth Divisions, apart from the twelve years after 1938 when they failed to secure re-election. At the end of March there was an important match at home to Swindon just at the time when a spate of injuries hit the first team. Even at the start of the week preceding the match against Swindon it appeared as if I was going to play. On the Wednesday Gerry Summers called me to one side and told me that I would be in the team on Saturday. He suggested that I should telephone my parents to see if they wanted to come down. In the course of an excited telephone conversation they, as expected, said that there was no doubt that they would be there. Everything was set, until the manager changed his mind on Friday.

I was absolutely devastated. This was the first setback I had received and showed me what a cruel game football can be. I just could not believe that an eighteen-year-old should be treated in this way. To be told that I was playing, to have arranged for the family to come down to watch my full League début, and then to have it dashed from me at the last minute left me inconsolable. I had trouble blinking back the tears as Gerry Summers explained that he felt the occasion would be too much for me and that it would have meant playing out of position as full back John Sharpe was injured. I was convinced that if I could play at centre-half I would have no trouble in coping with full back. The manager did not see it that way and opted for Charles Young to make one of his few appearances in the Gillingham first team. Eventually, seeing my disappointment, he tried to ease the pain by saying that he might use me as a substitute. It was a gesture, but one that I immediately rejected. If I was not going to play, I did not want to be on the bench.

I was captain of the youth team by this time, and I said that if I could not play in the first team I would rather go to play with my own team who were doing well in the South-east Counties League. And that is what I did. I went to Portsmouth having dashed to a telephone box along the road to catch my mum and dad before they left home to travel to Gillingham. I think they felt as bad about it as I did. Gillingham drew the match against Swindon 2–2, finished fourth in the table at a time when three teams gained promotion, and have not yet managed to get out of the bottom two divisions. Once again, my youth team finished sixth in the South-east Counties League.

The end of the season was a good time to look back at what had happened to me over the previous two years and to assess my situation. Although I had not played in the Football League for Gillingham I had played for England, and on the whole, I was satisfied with my progress. I think it was fair to say that I felt that I was on course at that stage of my career. The fear that I had encountered at the start of that season, namely that I might not be offered terms, proved to be groundless as I was signed on as a full professional. There had been a little bit of talk in the press about the possibility of a big club coming in for me and that, along with the England appearances, helped give me some bargaining power when it came to negotiating my first contract. I can remember Gerry Summers conducting those negotiations by saying that he was prepared to offer me this and that. I sat there listening before plucking up courage to say that the terms were not good enough. I was even going to be worse off because the club would no longer pay for my digs. We sorted it out eventually so that, taking an overall view of my two years by the Medway, I reckoned that my report would read as better than merely satisfactory.

I felt happy when I returned home to the North East for the summer. Janet had just left school at sixteen and we spent most of the summer together. It could be said that we were a bit serious by the time I returned to Gillingham for pre-season training. By now, though, I could afford a car which made it easier to return home more regularly. I travelled thousands of miles up and down between Gillingham and Newcastle. It helped that we had just signed Micky Barker from Newcastle United, and he was very homesick for the North East. He wanted to get back at every opportunity and I was happy to go with him.

Not that I had many problems at Gillingham, because it was at the start of the 1979–80 season that I made my début with the first team. Gerry Summers told me during the pre-season build-up that I would be starting the season in the side. I did not bring up the fact that he had told me I was in the team once before. It was particularly ironic that one of the reasons he had given for not playing me before was that I would have been playing out of position. Now he told me that I was going back into midfield. We had a few practice matches to get settled in and then we played Luton in a League Cup tie. In those days the first round of the competition was played over two legs before the League season got under way. Luton was a good Second Division team with a few full international players to call on, but we beat them 3–0 at home and then got a 1–1 draw in the second leg at Kenilworth Road to win 4–1 on aggregate.

That match had been on a Wednesday evening and, while it was important to play in these competitive matches with the first team, the major milestone was reached the following Saturday when I made my début in the Football League. We went to Blackpool, then managed by one of England's heroes of the 1966 World Cup, Alan Ball. My parents came down to Bloomfield Road to watch, but they did not see a fairy-tale start to my career as a League player. We lost 2–1, and what I remember most about the match was getting flattened by their goalkeeper, Tom McAllister. Fuelled by youthful enthusiasm, I went to challenge for a ball that I probably had no hope of getting to and he knocked me spark out. When I came round I played on for a few minutes before being taken off and my mate Billy Hughes came on as substitute.

The next season when we went to Blackpool again, we lost 4–0 in a match in which Alan Ball was actually playing. I had watched the 1966 World Cup final on television and had followed his career with Arsenal and Everton. He was, by now, getting towards the veteran stage but he was brilliant that day. The manager had told me to get in against him and to be aggressive. I seldom needed encouragement to do that, but it was to no avail as the great little man, past his best or not, taught me a lesson in football that day. Every time I had tried to do something against him he must have sensed that I was still very naïve, and exposed me with a single touch as I rushed in. He had time on the ball because I could never get close enough, teaching me a lesson that I will never forget.

By then I had played against another member of the England side that had won the World Cup. Martin Peters was playing for the Norwich City team that we drew with in the second round of the League Cup in my début season. We actually took the lead against the First Division side in the first leg at home before they equalised. The second leg was a memorable occasion for me because after half an hour we were leading 2–0, with me scoring both the goals. There was a genuine chance of upsetting a side from the top division, before their extra class told and they beat us 4–2. Little did

I know then that in a few years time Carrow Road would be my home ground.

For me, life was good. I established myself in the first team, I was even scoring a few goals, and in no way did I feel out of my depth. However, personal success was not matched by team success because we spent most of that season struggling in the lower half of the League table. We had a good start to move up among the leaders with only one League defeat in the first eight matches, in addition to our efforts in the League Cup. Then, around the turn of the year, we played thirteen matches with only one victory so that relegation was a distinct possibility. We managed to lift ourselves to sixteenth place, but with four sides facing the drop we were only three points clear of Bury who went into Division Four at the end of the season.

Gillingham did not win any trophies that season, but the Bruce mantelpiece was well endowed. Towards the end of the season I made a clean sweep of the club's awards by being named as the Player of the Year, the Young Player of the Year and the Players' Player of the Year. I felt I had arrived. I had played most of the season in midfield, but I began to get a hankering for the centre-half berth again. It was good experience to be involved in the midfield action, but I felt that I needed to get back to the centre of the defence if I was to make the most of the potential I felt I possessed. Fortunately, the manager saw it that way as well because I played as centre-half in the last few matches of the season.

In any football club it is the manager and coaching staff who have the biggest influence on the way a player develops. That is the way it should be because they are being paid to fulfil that function. However, senior players can make an impression on youngsters and I found that I spent a lot of time with people like Terry Nicholl, the brother of Northern Irish international Chris Nicholl who later became Southampton's manager, and Damien Richardson who had himself played for the Republic of Ireland. I enjoyed playing with them and listening to them talk because I felt I could learn from their experience in the game. I also used to go up to London to watch and learn from football in the First Division. I wanted the chance to be on the same stage, and if it turned out that I was not good enough, I would have been happy to return to the lower divisions. What I wanted was to prove it one way or the other.

It would have been good to have a few more older players around to help with this learning process. Most clubs will attract the fading stars who come from big clubs to play out their remaining years in the game. This did not seem to happen at Gillingham who were the only club in Kent and appeared to be out on a limb. During my time there the only one who gravitated to the Priestfield Stadium was Terry Cochrane. A Northern Irish international winger, he had gone off the rails a little bit but came to Gillingham from Middlesbrough and for a while really excited the players and the crowd. He was, though, perhaps not an ideal example for the younger players to follow. In one game that I remember he became so fed up with the lack of service he was receiving that he went off the pitch, climbed over the perimeter wall and sat in the front row of the stand. When asked what he was doing he replied that he had been a spectator for most of the game so thought he might as well watch in comfort!

Terry Cochrane came to Gillingham as a signing by Keith Peacock. He had taken over as manager in July 1981 when the unfortunate Gerry Summers got the sack. My second season in the first team was scarcely better than the first in terms of team performance. We finished fifteenth in the table after an unbeaten run of eight matches towards the end of the season, but that was absolutely necessary as, this time, we were only two points clear of a relegation spot. Probably what put Gerry on the slippery slope was a defeat in the second round of the FA Cup at the hands of near neighbours Maidstone United. Maidstone were at that time an ambitious non-League club, and they took much delight in holding us to a goalless draw in the first match. We went to Maidstone for the replay and

School,
Monday.

Dear Mrs. Bruce,

Thanks a lot for washing the green strips. I know Emerald green is probably your favourite colour — but you shouldn't have gone to so much bother.

However, when Stephen's playing for Manchester United I don't think you'll have the bother of washing his strip!

Thanks again.
M. Bell.

First words of encouragement from Michael Bell, my schoolmaster at Walker Gate Primary School, 1970.

Walker Gate Primary Under 11's, with me holding my first football trophy, the Bagnell Cup. Michael Bell can be seen behind.

Benfield Comprehensive Under 16's, 1974.

Benfield Comprehensive Under 19's, 1976.

One of my first appearances for
Gillingham, 1978.

Janet and I celebrating: I have just been awarded
Player of the Year 1978–9 for Gillingham.

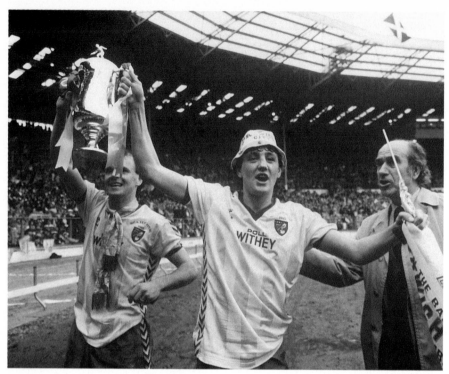

Victory for Norwich in the Milk Cup, 1985.

The Norwich team that won the 2nd Division in 1986.

Captaining the England B team against Malta at the Ta'Qali stadium in Valletta, 1987.

The family: Janet and I with Amy and Alex, three months before my transfer to Manchester United in 1987.

Sharing the Charity Shield with Liverpool at the beginning of the
1990–91 season.

Alex Ferguson (centre) congratulating Clayton Blackmore (left) and
myself for scoring the goals against Montpellier that took us to the 1991
European Cup-winners' Cup semi-final.

Holding the European Cup-winners' Cup in 1991; a triumphant moment.

after extra time the tie was still awaiting its first goal. It came in the second half of the second replay back at Gillingham, and was quickly followed by another. Both were scored by Maidstone and we were out of the Cup.

That second replay was the first time I had played in an FA Cup tie. Although I was a regular in the League team, I was not in the team that had gone out of the Cup to Wimbledon in the first round in 1978–80, and I was involved in neither the first-round tie against Dagenham in 1980–81, nor the first two games against Maidstone. I survived the indignity but Gerry Summers did not. Keith Peacock had made football history by being the first substitute to come on in a League match while playing for Charlton, for whom he made over five hundred appearances in the League. At the end of his playing days he had gone out to the United States as assistant manager with Tampa Bay Rowdies, before returning to England to take over at Gillingham. As his assistant he appointed Paul Taylor who had been a player at Southport when I was there on trial. It fascinates me to see how small the football comunity is. It is not a good idea to cross people unnecessarily, for you tend to come across them again when the world has turned a few more times.

Keith Peacock's first season in charge saw a change in fortune. Instead of just missing relegation, we came within seven points of promotion in sixth place. We also had a reasonable run in the FA Cup, when we took replays to get past both Plymouth Argyle and Barking before we beat Second Divison Oldham Athletic in the third round. We then got a draw to play First Division West Bromwich Albion in the fourth round at home. There were sixteen thousand people there to see us go down by the only goal of the game but, again, I had enjoyed the opportunity of playing against a top team.

By now I had played three seasons in the Third Division. I felt I had been improving all the time but there was a danger that my progress might stagnate if I stayed too long at this level. I realised that it is possible to become a good Third and

Fourth Division player rather than using the experience to go on to better things. I had always hoped to become something better than a player in a lower division, yet I was naïve enough to think that if a top club wanted to buy me, they would just come in with an offer that would be accepted and I would be on my way up the ladder. I kept signing contracts with the promise that if Gillingham got an offer they would keep me informed. To this day I am not sure that the club kept its promise. I was attracting quite a bit of attention and I knew there were a few big clubs looking seriously at me. Whether there was anything more substantial than press speculation I did not know. This was when I felt let down. I suspected that offers had come in and had not been accepted, but I was never told about them.

I knew I had been playing well, so I began to wonder whether it was going to happen or not. Perhaps I had played my best football but my best was not good enough to take me to the top. I wondered whether I had shot my bolt. I remembered Billy Hughes who had set out with such talent and promise as a sixteen-year-old. Everybody was putting in bids for him then, but by the time he had got to his early twenties he had begun to just ease off the pace. He could not get into the Gillingham team, struggled at Crystal Palace and Wimbledon, and had drifted out of the game. I had a big fear of that happening to me. I suppose that I started to drift myself for a season or two. Without wishing to sound big-headed, I knew I could play at this level and needed a new challenge to stimulate me.

The event that got me thinking positively again took place in February 1983. Janet and I got married. In spite of the fact that we had just bought our first house, we decided that I should take a bit of a gamble by letting my contract with Gillingham run out at the end of the following season. This would leave me free to look for another club higher up the scale, or, alternatively, would leave me free to see my career go up in a puff of smoke if things did not work out! The offer of a new contract was there, but I decided not to sign it. We were having an average season in the League, always hovering around the middle of the table, but had got through to the third round of the League Cup, then known as the Milk Cup. We were beaten 4–2 at home by a star-studded Tottenham side, but it had once again given me the urge to play every week in such company and not leave my glimpse of a big occasion to the vagaries of a cup draw.

By the middle of April, there was nothing to play for in terms of League matches and the season appeared to be moving towards an untroubled close. It was then that there was a dramatic break in the pattern of my life. I had always liked to think of myself as a competitive player who gave his all. Never would I describe myself as a hard man, because I cannot stand the way some players try to make up for a lack of ability by kicking everybody in sight. When I was young my enthusiasm sometimes ran away with me, but even then my most serious crime was nothing more than excessive enthusiasm. Nowadays, my colleague at Manchester United Paul Parker says he remembers me having a bit of a reputation when he was playing for Fulham and I was with Gillingham. That was as a result of what happened in my first season. I was suspended by the end of September and finished the season with a record number of forty-six disciplinary points. If I had come up before the disciplinary commission any more times I think they might have shot me! I like to think that I have learned from those early days, even if I was the first man to be sent off when they brought in the ruling about professional fouls. I am proud of neither record and would rather be remembered as a decent footballer than as a hard man.

It was just a case of being an enthusiastic youngster going in recklessly for challenges when I stood no chance of getting the ball. I felt that if I did not go for it I was not giving my all for the team. It could have been me who invented the old joke about the referee who complains about a late tackle only for the offending player to protest that he got there as soon as he could! At one stage I got five bookings in succession and was the first player to reach forty disciplinary points without getting sent off. That shows that there was nothing malicious about my game; I was merely determined to compete.

On 9th April 1983, the day on which Corbiere won the Grand National at Aintree, we had a match at home against Newport County. Their attack was led by a tough old professional by the name of Tommy Tynan. He had been in the game a long time and had played for different teams, scoring goals wherever he went, but on this occasion he did not score. We were 2–0 up by half-time, after I had scored the second goal from the penalty spot. In the second half, Tommy Tynan hit me with his elbow in an off-the-ball incident. It was all of thirty seconds later that the ball was thrown in to him in the eighteen-yard box and bounced in front of the two of us. He had just hurt me and, for the only time in my career, I tried to hurt him, aiming a kick at him. He saw me coming, he lifted his leg and I got a glancing blow on the ball but followed through to kick straight on to the bottom of his foot.

I knew my leg was broken as soon as I went down. Bill Collins, who had been so good to me when I had first arrived at Gillingham, was first on to the pitch to see what was wrong. I told him my leg was broken but he did not believe me until I let go of it slightly and it gave way at the shin. He knew straight away that it would not need an X-ray to diagnose what was wrong. It might have been my own stupid fault, but that did not ease the devastation. However strong-minded you are, at such a moment any footballer has to ask himself whether that is the end of his career. So many do not come back after breaking a leg.

As I was being loaded on to the stretcher to be carried off, Janet had moved down to the side of the pitch by the players' tunnel. She knew what was wrong and how it had happened. Good, honest Geordie woman that she is, she offered her sympathy to me in phrases like 'You stupid idiot. What did you want to go and do a thing like that for?'. I was in too much of a state of shock to hear exactly what she was saying, but I do not think the Gillingham fans realised that these were terms of endearment. At least I think they were terms of endearment! Fortunately this was the only serious injury I have received in my career. I have broken my nose a few times and suffered all the cuts and bruises that go with the job, but that day taught me a lesson that I have never forgotten.

I have been lucky not to suffer more serious injuries in my career and I suppose that in a way I was even lucky with the timing of breaking my leg. In one way it came at a bad time in that I had just got married, had just bought a house, and was determined to leave my contract. On the other hand it came near the end of the season. It meant that I had the summer to recover from it. I was in plaster up to the thigh for two months but as soon as I got the all-clear from the specialist I worked really hard at getting back to my former level of fitness. Despite my efforts, I still had to wait six and a half months before I could play again. I was eased back in by coming on as a substitute at the end of September and played my first full game again on 1st October 1983. My contract was up at the end of the season so I needed to prove that I was back to my best and had something to offer a top club.

I have said that I was not prepared to trust in luck when it came to cup draws to help my career. However, it was exactly that necessary piece of good fortune that played such a significant role when I got back into the Gillingham side. I was still on the sidelines when the club was knocked out of the Milk Cup by Chelsea, but returned in time for our success in the FA Cup in our games against AP Leamington, Chelmsford and Brentford. The draw had been kind to us all the way through but now we, and I, wanted to be paired with a big club. Everton were one of the biggest. They had players of international stature right through the team which was one of the most formidable in the land at the time.

This was the chance for which I had been waiting ever since I had got back into the side after my injury. I knew that my leg had not suffered any lasting damage and I was back somewhere near my best form. But if I had been playing well before, it transpired that I was saving my best performance for the visit to Goodison Park. I felt that personally I had played a major part in securing a goalless draw. In the replay at Gillingham I played well again. By holding the mighty Everton to another goalless draw we attracted a fair bit of media attention. People were asking how Gillingham could keep an attack that included the likes of Scottish internationals Graham Sharp and Andy Gray, along with Irishman Kevin Sheedy and another renowned goal poacher, Adrian Heath, off the score-sheet for two games in succession. Whether it was justified or not, I was given most of the credit. It felt just like the old days in the youth team when I had the chance to respond positively when playing against big-name players.

We won the toss to stage the second replay at Gillingham. Apart from plenty of media attention, word had obviously got around within the game because there were at least half a dozen managers from First Division clubs at the Priestfield Stadium to watch. I did not have as good a game this time and we lost 3–0. Everton went on to win the Cup that year and the European Cup-winners' Cup the following season. We returned to Third Division action and I just wondered if my chance had come and gone. No offers came in and, although Gillingham were still offering me new contracts, I felt a bit let down at that point.

As a twenty-three-year-old I wanted some guidance as to how best to proceed. I did not really feel that Keith Peacock, for whom I had played loyally for a number of years, had my best interests at heart. Of course he has to put the club first, but I got the impression that he was more interested in keeping me as a player who was likely to give him the sound defence that would keep him in a job. He knew that I wanted to advance in the game, and that if I remained at Gillingham as a dissastisfied individual, I was unlikely to give of my best. When that happened I would not be as valuable to the club, either as a player or as a saleable asset. There comes a time when it is in everyone's interest for a player to move on. I felt then that that time had come, yet there was no positive reaction from the manager.

Perhaps no firm offers came in for me. However, I had every reason to believe that Newcastle, among others, were interested. I know that because the manager at St James's Park, Arthur Cox, actually telphoned me to see how I would feel about a move to Tyneside. How would any Geordie feel about playing for Newcastle? Is the Pope a Catholic? Keith Peacock always denied the offer from Newcastle, but he must have known what it would have meant to me to go home. Unfortunately, Arthur Cox left Newcastle that summer to go to Derby County, so nothing materialised. I had freedom of contract and believed strongly that, at the least, I should have been told about Newcastle's approach.

There was nothing that could be done about that situation, but I had to get something sorted out. The first club on the telephone with serious ideas about offering me a contract was Norwich. Their manager, Ken Brown and his assistant, Mel Machin gave me the impression that they were very keen for me to go there. They told me that they had watched me on numerous occasions and I could tell that they genuinely wanted to take me into the First Division as a player for Norwich City. They asked me to Norfolk for the weekend to have a look around. From my first contact with Ken Brown I knew there was something there that attracted me to Norwich. I also liked the idea of playing alongside the England defender Dave Watson and goalkeeper Chris Woods who were both Norwich players at that time. I had the chance to see Terry Venables at Queen's Park Rangers and Bobby Gould telephoned me with a view to getting me to Coventry. I told him that I had set my mind on Norwich so he graciously backed off and wished me luck in my career.

I went up to Norwich again to negotiate personal terms. Because I was so keen to go there and they were so keen to have me, these did not take long to agree. Gillingham were not so easy for Norwich to do business with. They quoted a figure of £200,000 from which Keith Peacock was not inclined to budge. No club would pay that, so they had to go to a transfer tribunal to arrive at a reasonable price. I was very grateful for the introduction of the tribunal system, otherwise I could still have been with Gillingham to this day.

I took my father-in-law Les Smith and brother Ian with me to the tribunal which is, in itself, a strange set-up. On the one hand you have the club wanting to buy saying you are perhaps not as good as they thought and on the other, the club you are leaving praising you to the heavens. Sir Arthur South, the chairman of Norwich, was obviously trying to get me at a knock-down price as good business practice demands, but it did not make me feel too good when he questioned my worth with such conviction. The tribunal eventually set a figure of £75,000 to be paid immediately and stated that a further three payments each of £20,000 were to be made after periods of twenty-five matches. Providing I played seventy-five times for Norwich, Gillingham would receive £135,000 in total. However, that would take at least one and a half seasons and I felt that they could have done better for themselves if they had been prepared to compromise.

I left the tribunal with my future still far from decided. Norwich had yet to accept the valuation and Sir Arthur South, who I have since come to know well and like a lot, gave the impression that all was not done and dusted. He came up to my brother and father-in-law and said bluntly, 'Is this fellow any bloody good?' He was told that I could play a bit. 'That's just as well, because he's costing us an awful lot of bloody money!' This at a time when transfers were calculated in several hundred thousand pounds more than mine without the blink of an eyelid. I went back to Newcastle worried that Norwich might not meet the stipulated valuation. There was still a bit of haggling to be done, but eventually Ken Brown telephoned to say that all was agreed. I went to Norwich to finalise personal terms and on 24th August 1984 my transfer was registered.

The chairman at Gillingham, Mr Cox, had always said that if they ever got £200,000 for me he would buy me a new car as a leaving present. That did not happen, of course, but I still wonder whether they did ever get any firm offers of that magnitude. It was only recently that I heard that George Graham had tried to buy me when he was at Millwall. I do not really believe that they did as well for themselves or for me as they could have done. It was a sad episode in my time at Gillingham because I had genuinely enjoyed the whole experience there. It taught me to take nothing for granted as I moved up the ladder, while to have played through two seasons trying to avoid relegation really taught me what pressure there is in football. To leave with that little bit of a bad taste upset me. I wanted to depart without tarnishing the happy memories I held of the place and the people. However, that phase of my career was now behind me. After some two hundred matches wearing the royal blue shirt of Gillingham, I was about to pull on the yellow of Norwich City Football Club to begin my career as a player in the First Division.

Chapter Four

From the very first contact I had with Norwich I had been made to feel welcome and wanted. It was a First Division club, but it was also a friendly club. Who knows, there might have been other, bigger clubs to which I could have gone at that time, but it was important to me to go into a welcoming atmosphere. That was certainly what I encountered at Carrow Road. I remember driving up to Norfolk with Janet, who was seven months pregnant, and thinking that this was the chance I had always wanted. In such circumstances there are always mixed emotions. Excitement, anticipation, a few nerves. They were all there as we made our way along the A11. It had not taken more than about half an hour to discuss personal terms with the financial director, Mr Robert Chase, who was later to become chairman. We had sold our house in Gillingham, were waiting to buy one in Norfolk, and I was committed to Norwich.

I had played in that League Cup tie at Carrow Road in 1979, when scoring my first two goals in senior football meant that I had happy memories of the ground which was always regarded as pleasant rather than daunting. There was the impression that Norwich were looking ahead to greater things rather than dwelling on what was a fairly modest history. What excited me as well was the fact that they had the then England centre-half, Dave Watson playing for them and it would be good to be able to measure myself against him. There was also a promising nucleus of players all over the pitch with the likes of John Devine, John Deehan, Keith Bertschin, Mark Barham who had been included in international squads with England, and goalkeeper Chris Woods who was soon to play for England. Add to those the likes of Mick Channon and Asa Hartford and there was the basis for a fine side.

This team was coached by Mel Machin who had a big influence on my career at Norwich, just as Bill Collins had at Gillingham. Whereas Bill had spent a lot of time in helping me to develop in size and in strength, Mel Machin considered me to be overweight. In fact, I weighed in at twelve stone six pounds which was not excessive as I was almost six feet. However, Mel decided that I would be put through the mill to shed those pounds which he thought would make the difference between my being a Third Division and a First Division player.

We were to have four days of training before we left for a pre-season tour of Scandinavia. These must have been the most difficult four days I had ever suffered. Rather than losing a few pounds, I thought I was going to lose my life. I remember arriving home after training and saying to Janet that I might have made a mistake in jumping up two divisions. I really did not think I could cope with the extra demands of the training. Our training ground was at the University of East Anglia where I was certainly given an education in football. I discovered that it was not only the skills and the tactics which were of a higher level than I had experienced before.

Mel Machin ran us and ran us and then ran us some more. On one of these training runs I was just a few yards in front of the backmarker, John Deehan, as we crossed a small stream. He was exhausted as well, and collapsed into the water. I was so tired that I did not have the energy to go back all of ten yards to pull him out. As I reached the reserve team coach, Dave Stringer, I just managed to gasp out that he ought to go and see that John Deehan was all right. More than a little alarmed at the prospect of our top goal-scorer slowly drowning, he raced back to find him. Having rescued him and slung him over his shoulder, Dave Stringer still managed to overtake me before we got back, I was moving that slowly by then. I honestly thought that I would not be able to handle such a regime.

It made quite a change for someone who had, at one time, been a skinny little weed to find himself with a weight problem. However, by the time we reached the start of the League season, Mel had worked me so hard that I felt in really good shape, having shed the extra pounds. For the first time, I was made aware by both him and the physio of things like a proper diet. The facilities and attitudes were on a higher plane altogether than those I had been used to. It dawned on me fairly early on that I had to adopt the same highly professional standards as the players I was now with. I was impressed by the way in which the better players took so much pride in personal performance. They would work on their technique sometimes late after training. The likes of Chris Woods and Dave Watson would make immense efforts to work on their game, leaving nothing to chance where sensible practice was concerned. This was the main difference between life at Gillingham and life at Norwich. It was a difference that I had not expected, but with which I quickly came to terms.

We had played about a dozen matches on our pre-season tour before the time came for the opening of the League campaign. There could not have been a bigger match for me to begin my First Division career – at home to the League champions and European champions, Liverpool. Carrow Road was packed, the atmosphere was electric and the temperature in the eighties. There was a fair bit of attention focused on me as I was the only new signing by the club that summer. Everybody had tried so hard to make me welcome that I wanted to make an impact in my first match. I think it is fair to say that I did not go unnoticed on my début.

After only twenty seconds Liverpool attacked down the flank. Paul Walsh whipped in a cross, I went for it, only to power a diving header past Chris Woods into my own net. I remembered the momentary stunned silence of the twenty-two thousand people in the crowd and the looks of disbelief on the faces of colleagues and opponents alike. It was not a deflection or a ricochet, it was a full-blooded, well-directed, thumping header. As I picked myself up to my knees, all I could say was, 'You'll have to pick that one out, Woodsy!' Janet was watching from the stand and the shock was too much for her. It was not long before our son, Alex, was born prematurely.

Not more than twenty minutes after this unfortunately spectacular opening Kenny Dalglish moved menacingly down the middle. As Dave Watson closed in to tackle, Dalglish made to shoot before pulling the ball back on himself and trying to curl one into the top corner with his left foot. I attempted to get back on the line to knock it out, but only succeeded in helping the ball into the net. Everybody put it down as a great goal by Dalglish whereas, if I am honest, I got the final touch to that one as well to register my second own goal within twenty minutes of being a First Division player. Fortunately we got back into the game to draw 3–3, and I like to think that I played a decent part in the rest of the match. The press were reasonably fair, describing my nightmare beginning but commenting that I had shown a bit of character to get stuck in for the remainder of the ninety minutes. At least I had time to make amends for my beginning. There was, apparently, a glimmer of hope for the new boy.

We followed up that game on the Saturday with a mid-week game against Coventry City at Highfield Road. Again, I felt as if I was playing my part in keeping out the Coventry attack as we went into the last five minutes with the score 0–0 when I made a terrible mistake. Dave Bennett was on his way to taking the points when Chris Woods pulled off a marvellous save to deny him and save my blushes. Once the dust had settled, I thought back over my first two matches in the top division. In general I was quite pleased with the way they had gone, but I realised I had made two mistakes with the own goal against Liverpool and the error from which Chris Woods had extracted me at Coventry. It was obvious that, at this level, I had to improve to prevent any elementary gaffes appearing in my game. Not only were they more likely to be punished than they were at a lower level, but there was all the attendant publicity to highlight and magnify my every move.

It was as well that I realised that at this stage, and I am thankful that I reacted in the right way. I could have just put it down to bad luck and hoped that my fortune would change. On the other hand, a professional sportsman cannot base a career on luck, good or bad. I decided that I had to make sure such errors were kept to an absolute minimum. I worked hard on my game with support and encouragement from Mel Machin, as well as Ken Brown. The manager had been a centre-half himself, and had won FA Cup and European Cup-winners' Cup medals with West Ham and gained an England cap. He knew what was required and had a very cheerful philosophy. He would put his arm round me, sit and have a drink and tell me to forget any little mistakes that I had made rather than allow them to affect my game. 'Don't worry about it' was almost a catch-phrase of his. He was reassuring, while Mel Machin was the one who did the hard work with me on the training ground. It was a good pairing of contrasting individuals that so often makes the best management teams.

The main area that Mel homed in on was developing a partnership with Dave Watson. It was vital to establish this trust and understanding in the centre of defence and, fortunately, it was not long in coming. That allowed me to develop until I felt totally comfortable about playing week in, week out against some of the best sides and individuals in English football. I have always enjoyed this challenge. The bigger the names, the more I wanted to play. The fact that I was enjoying it meant that I was playing well, a fact supported by the reviews I was getting. The supporters and the press had warmed to me and I was revelling in my new life.

The League season was progressing satisfactorily with a position in mid-table seeming assured at that stage. We were progressing well in the Milk Cup too. The draw had been reasonably kind to us, with a two-leg affair with Preston in the second round when we won 9–4 on aggregate and I had scored in each leg to record my first goals for Norwich. In the third round we were held to a goalless draw at home by lowly Aldershot, but went there to win the replay 4–0. Before Christmas we had beaten Notts County 3–0 in the fourth round so, at the turn of the year, we were in the quarter-finals of the Milk Cup, we had the prospect of a third-round FA Cup tie against Second Division Birmingham City, and we were in the top half of the league table.

The FA Cup tie proved a tricky one. Birmingham were having a good season and had a long unbeaten run at St Andrews. They went on to gain promotion and gave us a real test. A goalless draw there was followed by a 1–1 draw at Carrow Road after extra time. The score was 1–1 again at St Andrews in the second replay, with both goals coming in extra time after the score-line had stood at 0–0 after ninety minutes. Eventually we came back to Carrow Road for the third replay and I scored a goal in the first half to see us through to a fourth-round tie at West Ham where we lost 2–1. During our marathon encounter with Birmingham we had played at Grimsby in the quarter-finals of the Milk Cup and had won 1–0. I had never before been involved in such cup exploits, except for the protracted tie against Everton in my Gillingham days. The cup run gave an impetus to the club and to the whole area. As a result of these games and the League outings at major grounds in Liverpool, Manchester, Sheffield and London, I realised what I had been missing in the lower divisions. I was loving my new life, and it was to get better.

The draw for the semi-final of the Milk Cup paired us in a two-leg meeting with our East Anglian rivals, Ipswich Town. We had lost a League match there on New Year's Day, and promptly went down 1–0 in the first leg of the semi-final at Portman Road. It could have been three or four because Ipswich played exceptionally well to give us a seeing-to not reflected in the score-line. However, John Deehan wiped out that deficit in the first half of the return at Carrow Road. It was a little fortunate in that it took a deflection on the way in to maintain his record of scoring in every round. Even so, the tie looked destined to go to extra time when we won a corner in the last few seconds of injury time. Mark Barham swung it into the crowded penalty area, it was my head that met it and Norwich were at Wembley. I think it is fair to say that my performances during the season had wiped out the memory of that own goal against Liverpool, but if there were any lingering doubts they were totally eradicated with that goal against our arch-rivals Ipswich in such an important game. East Anglia might not be known as an area that generates fervent support of football in the same way as some of the big cities, but it still meant everything to the supporters to win a derby match. I was the hero of all Norfolk.

Norwich had won the League Cup in 1962, before the final of the competition was played at Wembley. They beat Rochdale 4–0 in a home-and-away two-leg final. In 1973 and 1975 they had reached Wembley in the same competition and had lost 1–0 both times to Tottenham and Aston Villa respectively. A decade later everyone associated with the club and the supporters were looking forward to another big day out. It is always said that the League Cup is the poor relation to the FA Cup. While I understand that view, it could do nothing to dampen our enthusiasm now that we were in the final.

This was to be my first opportunity to play at the great stadium. I had been there on a couple of occasions as a spectator and had even performed at Wembley once before. Before the quiz buffs suggest that I played in the band or that I was at a dog show in the Wembley Arena, I should point out that I was there as a ball boy. Newcastle United played Manchester City in the League Cup final of 1974 and they had a ballot to provide six ball boys from the Newcastle Boys side and six from Manchester Boys. I was one of the lucky six from Tyneside and enjoyed a wonderful day out, even if Newcastle lost 2–1 with the deciding goal being an overhead scissors kick from Dennis Tueart. He was a Geordie by birth who had begun his career with Sunderland. By chance, our opponents at Wembley were to be Sunderland, just to give me, raised as a black and white Newcastle supporter, that extra little incentive if any was needed.

Two weeks before the final I had a big scare when I twisted my ankle in training. As a result I missed the League match before the final which happened to be a 3–1 home defeat at the hands of Sunderland. That reminded us we were in for a tough game at Wembley. Thankfully, I recovered in time to take my place in the heart of the defence for the game that really mattered. Just six months after being a Gillingham player I was to feature in a side appearing in a Wembley cup final. At Gillingham we might have won the Kent Senior Cup or something of similar stature, but my only real honour was to be named by the Professional Footballers Association in their Third Division representative side three years running. The team thus nominated never actually played, but at least I was gaining some recognition. Now I had earned my place in a team that was to take the field in a national cup final.

I used to room with John Deehan who had been a member of the Aston Villa team that had beaten Everton in the final in 1977. The night before our final, I asked him what it had been like. I wanted to know about the atmosphere, nerves – all about it. He admitted that he had remembered nothing at all about the big day. It had just passed him in a blur. He told me not to make the same mistake. He advised me to take everything in and remember it all, good or bad, because I might never get another chance to savour such a day. He was fortunate in that he was making a return visit and he was determined not to let this one pass him by.

It was about eight o'clock on the Sunday morning of the match when I was awoken after a fitful night's sleep by Janet on the telephone. I think all the girls had just got back to their hotel after a night out at Stringfellow's. They were determined to enjoy their trip to London, whatever happened in the game itself. I tried to take much the same approach, but even so I was more than usually nervous and tense. I wanted to relax and enjoy the atmosphere of a major occasion in football, but that was not simple. All the family came down to support me on my big day, finding it easy, as committed Newcastle supporters, to cheer on any team playing against Sunderland. For their part the Sunderland supporters were as vociferous as ever, bringing their famour Roker Roar to Wembley to create a wonderful atmosphere in opposition to what seemed like the whole of Norfolk, who had turned up to offer equally loud encouragement to Norwich.

To be fair, the game was never a classic by any stretch of the imagination. Having said that, it was very special for me, all the Norwich players and for everyone bedecked in yellow and green. I took John Deehan's advice and tried to take in everything. That included walking out on to the pitch before the start, where I was impressed by the quality of the surface which resembled a velvet green carpet with a three-inch pile, to just about every kick of the match itself. One kick I remember very clearly came from Asa Hartford in the second half. His free kick took such a deflection off the unfortunate Gordon Chisholm, the Sunderland defender, that it went down in the official records as an own goal. I also remember Clive Walker having the chance to score for Sunderland from the penalty spot. He missed and we won the cup with a score of 1–0

I had seen so many teams mount the thirty-nine steps to the Royal Box at Wembley to receive a trophy on television. I never thought it would happen to me but here I was, having not yet played in thirty First Divison matches, taking my place in the climb up the most famous stairway in football to receive my winners' medal. That was not all I collected, because I was also voted as the official Man of the Match and was presented with a silver salver in recognition of that. All this was happening in such a short space of time after leaving

Gillingham. The move had been a good one. The speed of it all was summed up by Jimmy Hill who was commentating on television. He claimed that he did not know who it was wearing the number four shirt for Norwich because, as far as he could tell, he had not seen me before and knew nothing about me! He knew me well enough by the end of the match to cast his vote for my getting that individual award.

They had waited a long time to have something to celebrate in Norwich and, although our official home-coming was on a foul night, they turned out in their thousands upon thousands to cheer us. In fact, it could be said that the celebrations went on a bit too long. We were exactly halfway in the League when we played at Wembley, and following our success we had two home games in which we beat Coventry and drew with Sheffield Wednesday. Then the rot set in. We suffered five successive defeats when we scored only twice, then beat bottom club Stoke City 3–2 away, before plunging into a run of three more defeats when we failed to score a single goal, followed by a goalless draw at home to Newcastle. Such a sequence of results sent us plummeting down the table to twentieth position. To conclude our season we had to go to play against Chelsea who were vying for a place in Europe.

It was a vile night at Stamford Bridge where the pitch was virtually waterlogged, but we knew that if we won we were likely to be safe from relegation. Asa Hartford scored for us and Mickey Thomas took a goal for Chelsea in the first half before I chose an opportune moment to score my first League goal for Norwich – in the last thirty seconds of the match and the season. On hearing the news that Coventry had been held to a goalless draw at Ipswich, we thought we were safe and I could celebrate another triumph in my career. Coventry would now need to win all three of their outstanding fixtures to overtake us. Since those days the rules have been changed so that all teams have to finish their League programme at about the same time. However, we were not unduly worried because the chances of Coventry gaining nine points from three games were remote, bearing in mind that they had taken only one point from their previous four matches. The first of those three outstanding matches was against Stoke, who were already down with our final opponents in the Milk Cup, Sunderland. Coventry won at the Victoria Ground thanks to a penalty from Stuart Pearce and Ian Painter's missing one in the last few minutes for Stoke. Had he found the back of the net, Coventry would have been down, but they then beat Luton at home with the only goal of the game – a late deflection of a Brian Kilcline shot – to keep their hopes alive a little longer.

By the time they reached their final match of the season, at home to the runaway champions, European Cup-winners' Cup winners and FA Cup finalists, Everton, I had gone back to the North East with my family for the summer. I had become an established First Division, player, I had been voted Man of the Match in a Wembley final, I had scored the goal that took us there and scored another that I thought had ensured our survival in the First Division and I had been voted Player of the Year. On 26th May I was sitting in a pub called the Wheatsheaf in Ponteland, near Newcastle, and felt confident that we had nothing to worry about. Coventry could not beat Everton.

At around quarter-past nine my father-in-law went to the telephone to find out the result at Highfield Road. When he came back to say that Coventry had won 4–1, the bottom dropped out of my world. After all the emotional experiences of the previous seven months, I now had another one to cope with. I was a member of a team that had been relegated. It was dreadful. After just one season in the top flight, and one that I had enjoyed so much, I simply could not come to terms with the fact that it was all over. Not only had I lost my chance to share a pitch with the best in England, I was also about to have the chance to play in Europe dashed from me. Not only was I hit because it would have been the first adventure into European competition for Norwich as we had qualified for the UEFA Cup by winning the Milk

Cup, but three days after Coventry beat Everton, the Heysel disaster took place and all English clubs were barred from Europe as a result.

My own form had stood up to the traumas of Norwich's slide down the table to the extent that the press was full of speculation about other clubs putting in offers for me. One report, I remember, concerned Tottenham who were supposed to have put in a massive bid. A couple of weeks later I received an extraordinary telephone call from Mr Robert Chase, who was by now the chairman of Norwich. He had taken over from Sir Arthur South during a boardroom reshuffle following the fire that had destroyed the main stand at Carrow Road. It was felt inappropriate that Sir Arthur, who was involved in the construction business, should preside over the club at a time when there was to be major building work carried out at the ground.

It was Mr Chase therefore who said that the club were delighted with the way I had played for them during the season and they would like to reward me by offering a new contract. My immediate thought was that if they were offering me a new contract after one season, something must be happening on the transfer market. With two years still to run, I expressed my thanks but explained that I did not want to extend my contract at that stage. Mr Chase then explained that they were not asking me to sign for longer, they just wanted to give me a pay rise in recognition of my efforts, and indicated that if I helped Norwich to get straight back out of the Second Division, there would be another review in a year's time. It was a fine gesture which I accepted without hesitation.

I must pay tribue to Norwich's management for the way in which they coped with the disappointment of relegation. So many clubs faced with a similar situation ruthlessly prune the playing staff to keep costs down and to realise as large transfer fees as possible. Norwich did not panic in that way. They retained the nucleus of the team which had, after all was said and done, won a trophy and had enjoyed a good season until the dramatic closing weeks. They even went out and bought players from the lower divisions who had done well without gaining recognition for steady progress. I like to think that they regarded me as an example of such players. My career had followed a similar pattern and they felt they had got good value from me. Now they turned to the likes of Mike Phelan and Wayne Biggins from Burnley, Dave Williams from Bristol Rovers and Kevin Drinkell who had a good goal-scoring record for Grimsby. These players just added a little extra depth to the squad as well as having plenty of experience of what was needed to succeed outside the First Division.

Fortunately, too, the people of Norwich did not turn their backs on us. Naturally they were not happy for the city to lose its representatives in the First Division, but they accepted the situation and there were no recriminations. The supporters had enjoyed their visit to Wembley for the final of the Milk Cup and had enjoyed the experience of winning. Norwich had a history of promotion and relegation and was, anyway, not exactly a hotbed of soccer tradition. There had been good times, and this was just a turn of the wheel that had resulted in a time to suffer a misfortune.

The players who had been part of the team that had won at Wembley and that had been relegated had two ways of reacting to the situation open to them. Presuming they did not immediately slap in a transfer request, they could either sit around moping about the injustices of life or role up their sleeves and show everyone what a stupid mistake it had been to allow the club to slip out of the top division. However well anyone had played as an individual, everyone felt guilty about the fact that we had gone down. Inspired by the example of the management, I am pleased to say that we adopted the latter course of action. We took the attitude that we had got ourselves into the unfortunate position in the first place, so it was up to us to get out of it as quickly as possible.

However, this did not mean that we got off to a very

good start. Of the first five matches that season, we won one, drew one and lost three. From then on we lost only three more matches before promotion was secured with a victory of 2–0 at Bradford City on 12th April. A week later we drew 1–1 with Stoke City to confirm that we would go up as champions. A Second Division Championship medal was not one that I had set out to win when I joined Norwich, but if we had to get out of that division we at least did it in style. We went through an unbeaten run of eighteen matches in the middle of the season that included ten successive victories. We had won 3–1 away at Oldham to go top for the first time, and stayed there until the end of the campaign.

During that winning run of ten matches we had earned ourselves a few bob because of the bonus system offered by Norwich at that time. The bonus increased in steps according to how many matches were won and such a long run was very profitable. We were due to move up another step if we won the eleventh match in that run, away to Barnsley. We were 2–1 up with only minutes to go when a lad called Gwyn Thomas hit a shot that cannoned back into play after hitting some part of the goal structure. Some people claimed that it had come off the crossbar, others that it had hit the stanchion in the back of the goal. The referee took the latter view, so we drew 2–2 and lost our increased bonus. I was standing only fifteen yards away from the incident, and to this day I could not be sure whether the shot went in or not.

When the pressure was off we lost a couple more fixtures, but finished the season seven points clear of Charlton and eight clear of Wimbledon, the other two clubs who had been promoted. On the last day of the season we beat Leeds 4–0 and I scored my eighth League goal of the season. After the match there were the usual joyous scenes as we were presented with the Second Division trophy. The home fans gave us a tremendous ovation as we did our lap of honour displaying the silverware. The large contingent of Leeds supporters gave us something other than a round of applause. Despite the fact that they had finished way down

STEVE BRUCE

the table, only seven points clear of a relegation spot, they appeared to resent the fact that we had done so well. It was a few years later, at the end of the 1989–90 season, that these same unruly elements among the Leeds supporters rioted in celebration of their team's promotion at Bournemouth.

We made quite a good defence of our Milk Cup as well in the 1985–86 season. I scored at Deepdale to give us a 1–1 draw in the first leg of the second-round tie against Preston. After going behind in the second leg at Carrow Road, we eventually won 2–1 before going to Luton to win 2–0 in the third round when I scored again. The fourth-round draw took us to the Manor Ground, Oxford, where we bowed out of the competition having lost 3–1 to the eventual winners. It was a different story in the FA Cup, where we were reminded of what was to await us on our return to the First Division. We went to Anfield to play Liverpool in the third round and were unceremoniously trounced 5–0. At least I got away without scoring an own goal.

In an attempt to compensate clubs that had qualified for European competition before the ban had been imposed, the Football League introduced a tournament called the Super Cup. Everton who had been champions and Manchester United, the FA Cup winners were involved. So too were Liverpool, runners-up to Everton in the League and Tottenham and Southampton who would have had places in the UEFA Cup. Added to that élite list were Norwich City, winners of the Milk Cup. Despite the good intentions there was no way that this competition could take the place of glamorous trips to play the best in Europe, and the public failed to give it the support it deserved. Or perhaps they did give it the support it deserved. Crowds were generally poor and interest could be gauged by the fact that the final was held over to the following season, when Liverpool thrashed Everton 7–2 on aggregate over two legs.

The six teams were split into two groups of three who played each other on a home-and-away basis. Our group included Manchester United and Everton, which at least ensured that we would have four opportunities to play in top company during the season. There were only ten thousand or so at Goodison Park when we went down to a goal from Gary Lineker in our first match against Everton, but we beat them 1–0 in the return at Carrow Road. We were leading 1–0 at Old Trafford in our game against Manchester United before Norman Whiteside scored from the penalty spot, but Everton beat Manchester United twice before we drew with them 1–1 at home to take our place in the semi-finals. Liverpool were our opponents and after drawing 1–1 at home we were leading 1–0 at Anfield before they scored three in the second half.

I had played in all these matches and, if they were not paramount on the agenda of any of the clubs involved, they did reaffirm my enthusiasm to get back to the top as soon as possible. I was twenty-five years of age as we prepared for our return to Division One. I had enjoyed the only season that I had played at this level and was determined to make the most of my next opportunity. I realised that I had left it late to get to the summit, and should perhaps have got away from Gillingham earlier. I also realised how fortunate I had been when Norwich got back immediately after the desperate disappointment of relegation at the end of my first season with them.

Whereas the club had held on to all its players when we went down, there were two significant changes to the playing staff before the start of the new season. Glasgow Rangers, under Graeme Souness, were beginning to raid the English League for top players. One of their first targets was our international goalkeeper, Chris Woods, who moved to Scotland for £600,000 where he established a new British record for a goalkeeper. Then, just before the start of the new season, my partner in the middle of the defence, Dave Watson, left. He was also a current international, and when Everton made a bid for £1.2 million, he returned to his native city of Liverpool. At the same time, Shaun Elliott was signed from Sunderland as a replacement before he, in turn, lost his place to Ian Butterworth, who had begun his career with Coventry City before a brief stay at Nottingham Forest.

It was a blow to lose Dave Watson, with whom I had worked out a good understanding and who I respected as a player and as a person. I had learnt a lot from him after changing the way I played to accommodate his play. At Gillingham, it was always me who took the big fellow in the opposition attack. At Norwich, that was Dave Watson's job and I was left to play the supporting role to him. It was a job I enjoyed and which helped to make me a better player in the years to come, when I would take on a similar sort of role with Gary Pallister at Manchester United. It had worked well at Norwich as Dave Watson had the slightly taller and definitely the stronger build.

He relished the physical challenge and, although I could look after myself, I missed having him around after he had left. In that first season back in Division One, we had to play Wimbledon whose attack was led by that always abrasive and physical striker, John Fashanu. He had written what was described as an 'exclusive' newspaper article about coming back to his old club where he was going to frighten the life out of me. I was interviewed before the game by the local radio station in Norwich and said that however much John Fashanu and Wimbledon ranted and raved and tried to enhance their tough, Crazy Gang image, there was nobody who could frighten me on a football pitch.

I was at home having something to eat on the Friday evening when the telephone rang. Janet answered it, and the caller asked for me. When she asked who it was, the caller said, 'Just tell him it's Fash.' A very clear and articulate voice greeted me, 'Brucey, it's Fash. What's all this I've just heard on the radio while we were travelling up here? Is that right what you were spouting about not being frightened of me?' I discussed the matter, saying that he should not have put his name to newspaper articles like he had as they were not good for the image of the game. After listening to what I had to say he just said, 'Well Steve, I can't wait to meet you by the far post tomorrow where we will mince heads' and put the phone down. I could not finish my meal and wished that my mate, Big Dave, was going to be alongside me the next day.

During the game there was an incident when the Wimbledon goalkeeper, Dave Beasant, punted the ball upfield and it bounced horribly between Fash and me. It was one of those where I had to just shut my eyes, stick my head in and hope for the best against a man who weighed in at twelve stone of muscle. The two of us were flattened by the impact before getting up and exchanging meaningful glances. For the rest of the game his big mate, Vinnie Jones, was going all over the pitch saying comforting things to me like 'You're going to die; he'll kill you!' If it never quite came to that, nobody enjoyed playing against Wimbledon who achieved results by being thoroughly competitive. At least they didn't win that day because it ended as a goalless draw. It should not have ended like that because I missed a penalty. I think I might have been looking over my shoulder as I ran up to take it, just in case Fash was still after me!

Dave Watson's departure resulted in another honour coming my way. His transfer was completed just before the start of the new season, at which time Ken Brown called me into his office and asked how I would feel about taking on the captaincy of the club. It was a challenge I eagerly accepted. I had skippered Gillingham on a number of occasions and I enjoyed the extra responsibility the job entailed. We might have lost a couple of internationals but we still had a good season. I gained a good deal of satisfaction from the fact that I captained Norwich to their then highest ever position in the League. We finished fifth having, for a heady seven days in October, actually been top of the League. In the end we had to settle for a place behind Everton, Liverpool, Spurs and Arsenal. And I have to admit it, Wimbledon were sixth. In fact, Everton won the title by beating us 1–0 at Carrow Road. At that time it was the closest I had been to the First Division championship.

I was feeling thoroughly contented with my lot. We had a nice house, Norfolk was a terrific place to live and a good area for the family to grow up in. By now we had a complete family, for in May of that year our daughter Amy was born. I got on really well with the supporters and it was obvious that the club was taking shape. Norwich had always been the club that had to sell to make ends meet, but they were good at what they did. Who could argue with them when you look at the players they have taken there, developed and then sold on? The scouting system was brilliant and they seldom made mistakes. Players generally did the business for them and, when the time came for them to be sold, it was usually at a handsome profit. The ground was being developed into a compact stadium, while we were always encouraged to play attractive football. The mix was good.

Much of the credit for that had to be given to Ken Brown and Mel Machin. I had the highest regard for Mel's qualities as a coach, even if he did work us into the ground. Even established players like Mick Channon and Asa Hartford came to Norwich and were prepared to work for Mel. Ken Brown was a lovely, charming, big fellow who had graduated into management from what was always known as the West Ham academy. He had arrived at Carrow Road as assistant to John Bond, but stayed to take over when the flamboyant Bond moved on to Manchester City. Ken Brown was very rarely ruffled and seldom lost his temper. Only once can I remember him getting really upset with us. That was when we lost that FA Cup tie to Liverpool 5–0 in 1986. It was never a good journey back from Liverpool, and it took near enough five hours. We usually had a drink or two on the coach but this time the manager put his foot down in the dressing-room. There would be no refreshments on the journey home, because we had done nothing to deserve such luxuries. From Anfield to the start of the M62 is all of five miles but, before we had reached the motorway, Ken had ordered the driver to stop and had gone into an off-licence to stock up for the journey. He did not stay angry for long, and appreciated a quiet drink himself.

The jovial Ken Brown made a good management team with Mel Machin, who was the disciplinarian of the pair. Ken was nobody's fool, but it was Mel who laid down the law and came up with some brilliant ideas on the training field. It was about the time that Mel left, to take over as manager at Manchester City, that things began to go wrong at Norwich. Dave Williams, who had been player/assistant manager at Bristol Rovers before joining Norwich, was added to the coaching staff while Dave Stringer was promoted to become chief coach. After such a good season the year before we found it hard to get going. The results never came for us and, instead of being in the top five, we could not get out of the bottom five.

In the October of that season I enjoyed one of my proudest moments in the game – and, at the same time, I experienced one of my greatest disappointments. I had been selected to go to Malta with the England 'B' party. The game did not gain a lot of press attention because, on the same night, England were beating Turkey 8–0 in a qualifying match for the European Championship at Wembley. Nevertheless, for those of us involved with the trip to Malta it was an important occasion. I am sure all of us saw it as a signficant step on the international ladder.

Bobby Robson was manager of the full international side at the time and, in the scheme of things, Howard Wilkinson was meant to be the manager of the 'B' team as internationals at the level were resurrected. However, he was also managing the Under 21 side which had a game the previous evening in Sheffield against Turkey. Bobby Robson therefore appointed another up-and-coming young manager to look after us in Malta. Graham Taylor was, of course, to get the number one job after Bobby Robson and it was here that he got his first experience of running an international side of senior players.

I remember quite clearly how he sat us down to announce

the team that would play in the Ta'Qali Stadium in Valletta. It was to consist of David Seaman in goal; Mel Sterland, Steve Bruce, Chris Fairclough and Mitchell Thomas; Steve McMahon, Craig Johnston and Ian Snodin; Adrian Heath, Mick Hartford and Kevin Brock. The substitutes were to be Ian Crook and Paul Parker. I was still enjoying the experience of being named in an England line-up for the first time since I was a teenager in the Youth Team when Graham Taylor made me really proud. 'Steve Bruce will captain the side.' To captain England at any level was an enormous honour that does not come the way of many footballers. I relished the idea when he suddenly shattered my big moment. For some reason, he added 'That is not my decision. It was decided before I had anything to do with this team.'

Why he felt compelled to make that comment I do not know. Even if he had not wanted me as captain, there was no need to undermine the authority that had just been given to me by announcing his thoughts in front of the rest of the team. I considered it a most unfortunate and unpleasant incident. Perhaps I should have made some comment myself, in private rather than publicly, to Graham Taylor, but I just wondered why he should have said such a thing. Anyway, such thoughts were put to the back of my mind as I got on with the job in hand. It was still a great honour to lead out a team wearing the white shirt emblazoned with the three lions of England. We won comfortably with goals from Mel Sterland and Mick Hartford while I thought I played well enough in a defence that shut out the Maltese attack. However well I considered I played, I had obviously not done enough to get Graham Taylor to change his view of me. His report cannot have been very flattering because when the next 'B' international came round, I was not even in the squad.

Many good judges have been kind enough to say that I should have gone on to play for England in international football. It has been a great disappointment to me that I have never been given the chance to prove myself one way or the other at that level. If I had been put in the team and failed, I could have accepted that I was not good enough. It is not knowing whether I was good enough or not that gnaws at my professional soul. Most of the time I subscribe to the view that what I never had, I will never miss. In darker moments I hanker for my career to have been completed, as it would have been with an international cap.

I once met Bobby Robson at a testimonial match in which I was playing with Bryan Robson. He came up to talk to Bryan before he turned to me, shook my hand and said that he had made a mistake in not capping me. He did not have to make such a remark, but it was kind of him to do so. When Bobby Robson was replaced as England manager by Graham Taylor, I knew that I had very little chance of gaining that coveted full international cap. Every time I was mentioned as a possible for inclusion by the press, my mind went back to the dressing-room in Valletta. Remembering his comment on the captaincy, I thought I would have to be playing better than Franz Beckenbaur and Bobby Moore combined to force my way into a team managed by Graham Taylor.

The irony of the situation is that there was an Englishman managing an international side that wanted to give me a full cap. I had a call from Jack Charlton to say that he had heard that my mother was Irish and, as such, I could qualify to play for the Republic of Ireland. He would have liked me to play for Eire if I wished to do so. Realising that my chances of playing for England were virtually non-existent, I would have jumped at the opportunity and appreciated being wanted for an international side. However, there was an insurmountable problem. By playing in that UEFA Youth Tournament in 1979, I was bound to England. If I had been dropped after the friendly in Brussels, I would have been clear, but once I had stepped out in the Olympic Stadium in Rome to play Italy in a competitive match, I had lost my chance.

It is a little hard to accept that nowadays you can play in full internationals for one country yet, providing they were not matches in a FIFA-regulated competition, you can then switch to play for another country under a flag of convenience. It is a ruling which would, theoretically, allow full England internationals to play for Nigeria in the World Cup finals of 1994 while I could not be considered for the Republic of Ireland in spite of my other cast-iron qualifications. That was even harder to accept when Dennis Irwin and Roy Keane came back to Old Trafford after their successful qualifying campaign for the World Cup with Eire in November 1993. I was pleased for them, but would have loved to be part of it. On the other hand, my frustration at not being involved was no greater than the disappointment of Paul Parker, Gary Pallister, Paul Ince and Lee Sharpe who had missed out with England, or Ryan Giggs with Wales, Brian McClair with Scotland, Eric Cantona with France, or Peter Schmeichel with Denmark.

Back at Norwich in 1987 we were not thinking about the World Cup, but we had other pressing domestic matters to consider. As well as making a poor start to the League season, we had been knocked out of the League Cup, after losing 2–1 to Second Division Stoke City. I scored what was to prove to be my last goal for Norwich that evening. It was a miserable confirmation of our form and I knew that things were getting a bit fraught before, on 7th November, we went to play Charlton and lost 2–0. That was when the chairman's patience ran out. Two days later he decided to sack Ken Brown. I felt bad about it because I had got on so well with Ken, and when he was sacked I felt guilty. The manager had been sacked because we were not getting results and the players had to take a certain amount of responsibility. Everyone felt for Ken Brown because he was such a gentleman. The man appointed to take over was Dave Stringer, but he was unable to effect an immediate change in our fortune. In his first match in charge we went down 4–2 at home to Arsenal.

Dave Stringer had only been managing the team for four matches when I must admit that I turned villain on him. Things had started to pick up slightly in that we had drawn 0–0 at Anfield against Liverpool, lost at home to Portsmouth, but went away to win 2–1 at Luton. I had been told privately by Mel Machin, by then manager of Manchester City, that he knew Alex Ferguson was showing an interest in me across the way at Old Trafford. He was looking for a centre-half, had watched me several times and was keen. Then, on the Saturday evening following our defeat by Portsmouth, I had a telephone call from Eddie Booth who runs a sports agency in Manchester. He said that he believed Manchester United were going to make an offer and wondered whether I would be interested in going to Old Trafford if they did. My reply was to the effect that anybody in the world would be crazy if they did not want to play for Manchester United, given the chance.

I also told him about a clause I had negotiated in my contract whereby any approach from a big club would be conveyed to me. If Manchester United or anyone else made a firm offer for me, I would hear about it soon enough. To be fair to Norwich, Mr Chase was as good as his word and he did inform me of a bid by Alex Ferguson. That clause had been included as a direct result of being messed about a bit at Gillingham. I wanted to ensure that I was to be master of my own destiny if a similar situation occurred again. It was not that I particularly wanted to leave Norwich. In fact, had a club like Manchester United not come in for me I would have been happy to stay there. Norwich had been good to me, and I had signed three contracts with them. However, when Dave Watson and Chris Woods moved on I realised that I was one of their big assets, otherwise they would not keep offering me the contracts. When I signed the last one I merely asked to be kept informed should a big club actually make an offer.

After speaking to Eddie Booth on the telephone when he had confirmed Manchester United's interest, I was so excited I could not settle. There followed what appeared to be the longest three weeks of my life. The press had been made aware that something was in the air and, because it involved Manchester United, it was big news by Monday morning. I went in to see Dave Stringer who, having just taken over as manager, did not want me to leave. The team were struggling, I was his captain and a key member of the side, and he wanted me to stay to lead the club through the battle against relegation. I appreciated his predicament and wanted him to do well in his job because I liked him as a person and I cared for Norwich as a club. However, I pointed out that I was as ambitious as the next man and I wanted to be kept informed of developments.

A week or so passed, we had gone to Luton and won and, while I was told that Manchester United had tabled a bid, there was a protracted negotiation over the fee. Norwich were holding out for £1 million while Alex Ferguson had offered £700,000. They were getting close, and I had said that I wanted to go because this was the biggest chance I was ever likely to get in my career. I did not want to be disloyal to Norwich, but I did want to take my chance. As the affair dragged on I went to see Mr Chase who told me that before any deal could be agreed on he had to contact Chelsea who apparently had first refusal on me. I said quite firmly that I did not want to go to Chelsea; I only wanted to go to Old Trafford. I had never been told about Chelsea, who had not put in a formal bid before. It was a chairman's informal agreement that should I ever become available, they would be told. Then Tottenham came into the reckoning as well, just to confuse the issue.

I was getting upset about the way the whole thing was moving. The supporters were, understandably, branding me as a deserter who gave not a moment's thought to Norwich's plight. To keep them happy, Mr Chase said that a replacement had to be signed before I would be allowed to go. Robert Fleck had been lined up from Rangers for £500,000, not as a direct replacement for me but as a signal to the supporters that the club was maintaining ambition. This meant I had to wait until he arrived, so I had to bide my time until that had happened. All through these two and a half weeks since I had first heard about United's interest, I had to keep persuading myself that perhaps something concrete would happen tomorrow, or tomorrow, or tomorrow. Tomorrow never came.

To add to the difficulties, I had been told that, as well as signing Robert Fleck, the club wanted to sign a replacement centre-half. John O'Neill, a powerful Northern Irish international was lined up to come from Queen's Park Rangers, but this was another piece to be fitted in to the jigsaw. This transfer negotiation was taking on all the complications of a property deal involving a chain of would-be purchasers, all of whom required sales of their own houses and mortgages to be fixed before the chain could be completed. In those situations, if one link in the chain is broken, a whole succession of deals falls through. It so nearly happened to me.

When I had spoken to Dave Stringer about the deals, he had insisted that whatever happened he wanted me to play the following Friday evening at Wimbledon. It was then that I did the dirty on him by refusing to play. I said that this had been dragging on for long enough. I was determined to join Manchester United and that I had played my last game for Norwich. If he insisted on naming me in the side to go to Plough Lane, I would invent a calf injury or a hamstring strain rather than playing. Manchester United wanted me for their game at Portsmouth on the Saturday and I was not going to risk the whole thing to play just one more game for Norwich.

After leaving him with that thought on the Wednesday, I had a telephone call from Alex Ferguson on the Thursday morning to say that he was pulling out of the deal. Negotiations had been dragging on too long and he was not prepared to wait any longer. I was shattered. In these circumstances the player is the one with most to lose yet he is the one who really gets least consideration. Even though Manchester United wanted me as their first choice, there were other targets for whom they would have gone quite happily. Norwich were keen on the money which would allow them to buy two players to replace me, but if I stayed I could help

STEVE BRUCE

their fight against relegation and there would be others who would buy me at a time that might suit Norwich better. To both parties I was a desirable commodity that they could take or leave. I had only one career, however, so for me it was a matter of the utmost importance. If I missed this chance I knew there would never be another to match it.

The reason given for Manchester United's pulling out was that Norwich had asked for a further £50,000. I could not believe what was happening. By now, Robert Fleck had arrived and so had John O'Neill. Those moves prompted us to put our house on the market and it had virtually been sold within an hour. Janet and I just sat there, dazed by events and wondering what to do next. I decided to go to the ground to reaffirm to Dave Stringer that I was unavailable for the Wimbledon game. I told him that, after what had occurred, I was in no state to play anyway and could not believe what was happening to me. I then asked to see Mr Chase. He was a Justice of the Peace and was down at the County court on magistrate's duty. His secretary telephoned through to the court to inform him of the situation with regard to my threatened personal strike. Within half an hour he was back on the telephone to say that he had spoken to Manchester United, the deal was back on and I was free to go.

At nine o'clock the move was off; by ten thirty I was being told that I was on my way for £825,000. Before there could be any further twists and turns in the story, I left for Manchester. I had to try to find a plane to take me from Norwich to Manchester in time to sign before any minds could be changed again and in time to make my début for United on the Saturday. I made it by the deadline of three o'clock, with little time taken over settling personal terms. I did not say so at the time, but I was prepared to accept anything they offered. Both Chelsea and Tottenham had offered me more money, but money did not come into it, I was so keen to become a player for Manchester United. As a boy I had always dreamed of such a moment – a moment that had so nearly passed me by.

It could well have passed me by if I had agreed to Dave Stringer's request to play at Wimbledon on that Friday night. Not only might Alex Ferguson have finally lost his patience over the protracted negotiations for good, but there was an incident in the Norwich match at Plough Lane which sent shivers down my spine. While I was travelling with Manchester United to make my début, John O'Neill was wearing what had been my number four shirt for Norwich. He had only been wearing it for twenty minutes when he was at the receiving end of what, for legal purposes, had better be described as a 'strong challenge'. It resulted in him suffering a knee injury which ended his career.

I felt desperately sorry for John O'Neill, and also felt a certain responsibility, albeit in an indirect and totally unwarranted way. Later, I went to play in his testimonial match and I know he does not include me among those he blames for the incident. As well as feeling sympathy for him, I would not have been human if I had not thought 'that could have been me'. If I had not stood my ground about not playing at Wimbledon, it could have been me on the end of that challenge. While I did not necessarily like what I did to Dave Stringer, who had a very difficult job to do, I had a young family to consider and the rest of my career to plan. At the very moment poor John O'Neill was being carried out of football, I was on my way to fulfil my dream and the prophecy of Mr Bell from Walker Gate Primary School. I was about to play for Manchester United.

Chapter Five

My transfer to Manchester United from Norwich represented the most traumatic three weeks of my life. The fact that it all happened just before Christmas made matters worse because we had no idea where we would be spending what is an important time of year for a young family. Would Santa be going down a chimney in Norwich or in Manchester? When the terms of the move were at last finalised, it was as though Christmas had come a few days early for me. On the occasion that Eddie Booth had telephoned me to ask how keen I would be on moving to Old Trafford, I had replied that I would be prepared to crawl on my hands and knees to go and play there. It was against my nature to kick up a fuss with Norwich, but I have never regretted making the best move I could have ever hoped for.

The transfer having gone through on Thursday, 19th December 1987, I travelled with the team to the South Coast to make my début at Fratton Park against Portsmouth on Saturday, 21st. It was then that the size and ambition of the club I had joined sank in. Until that point Norwich had played ten away-matches in the League and had lost seven of them. We seldom travelled hopefully. With Manchester United we won 2–1 on my début at Portsmouth and I thought it was a terrific result. That was until I encountered Alex Ferguson. He sat everyone down in the dressing-room and, although he did not start throwing things, I could tell from his manner that he was not happy with our performance. It was not enough merely to win; we had to win in that distinctive Manchester United style. Even though we had won, we had not passed the ball enough nor had we moved off the ball well enough. Generally, he was not a satisfied man.

A friend of mine drove me back to Norwich from Portsmouth to enable me to clear up a few things. The journey gave me time to reflect on what had happened. I knew that Norwich would have been delighted to have played away and won, even if the winning goal had been a dubious penalty decision, a fluke of a deflection or a stupid own goal. We would have been thrilled. Just as I had to raise my sights and my own standards when I moved from Gillingham to Norwich, so I had to raise them once again if I was to settle in in my new surroundings as a Manchester United player. The expectations and demands far exceed anything else to be experienced elsewhere. Everywhere we go it's a full house with players and spectators alike treating the game like a cup final. Everyone enjoys playing against and beating Manchester United. Apart from the chance of going back to Newcastle, it was always the first fixture I had looked for at the start of a season.

During my career I had never exactly enjoyed a steady, unspectacular début. My first outing wearing the famous red shirt of Manchester United was no different. With Gillingham I had been taken off after being knocked out by the Blackpool goalkeeper and I had marked my Norwich début with that own goal against Liverpool. For Manchester United I weighed in by giving away a penalty and breaking my nose. I must admit that I thought the penalty was a rather dubious decision. I was penalised for pushing while going for a header. Kevin Dillon beat Chris Turner from the spot. By that stage I had already suffered the broken nose in going for a corner. I remember winning the ball but taking a clout. While the general discussion about the game had not been too favourable, I got the seal of approval from my new manager. A tap on the backside and a nod was as much as I could expect from Alex Ferguson.

I had little time to know where I was, let alone to dwell on how I was doing. From Portsmouth to Norwich and from there to Manchester for Christmas. We were staying at the Amblehurst Hotel in Sale while waiting to find somewhere to live. The hotel was not really open for Christmas, but Mike and Inge, the proprietors who have since become good friends, made us feel really welcome. They tried to make it feel like home, while Boxing Day really was spent at home. We went to play Newcastle at St James's Park so the family did not have to wait to see me wearing the red shirt of Manchester United. Furthermore, if they had not yet come to terms with the idea of my being a United player it did not matter. Newcastle beat us 1–0. Then it was back to the Amblehurst to prepare for my home début.

I must admit to being a bag of nerves before that occasion. The match was against Everton with a crowd of forty-seven thousand in Old Trafford. I knew I was to be the centre of attraction. The club had paid a lot of money for me and this was the first chance most of the supporters had had to have a look at what they had paid for. I experienced a huge sense of excitement building up to the game, knowing that at centre-half I only had to make one mistake to expose myself to dreadful criticism. Not only did we win 2–1, but in the closing minutes I made a last-ditch tackle to prevent Graeme Sharp from a certain equaliser. That challenge seemed to win over the fans and I am pleased to say they have been on my side ever since. The support cannot be matched anywhere, so it pays to have them with you rather than against you. When I said that I had been prepared to crawl there on hands and knees, they realised what it meant to me to appear in their side and that got me off to a good start. I genuinely believed then, and still do, that Manchester United were the biggest club of them all and the best. By saying so in public I did not need much in the way of an introduction from public-relations consultants.

Not only did I have to win the respect of the supporters, I also felt it was necessary to win the respect of my new colleagues. It was a little nerve-racking going into a dressing-room that included giants in the game like Bryan

Robson, Jesper Olsen, Gordon Strachan, Norman Whiteside and Paul McGrath. When moving to a new club it is important to convince the players already there that you are good enough to fit in with them. I had little chance to train with them, only playing a gentle five-a-side before the game at Portsmouth and knowing some of their names only by having seen them on television. Now I had to make a place of my own in their company.

A lot of players arrive with exactly the same problems to overcome as I did yet they fall by the wayside. They never come to terms with the enormity of being a player with Manchester United. Just as I had felt earlier at Norwich, I was determined to enjoy the experience rather than to allow it to destroy me. I was going to go out and play the way I had all my career. Alex Ferguson had been prepared to pay the transfer fee because he liked what he saw with Norwich. It would be stupid to try and invent fancy aspects of play that were not in my natural game. If I gave one hundred per cent and enjoyed it, I figured that I would not go far wrong. It might always be a highly pressurised game when playing for a club like Manchester United, but if you do not enjoy playing you will never cope. I felt that I had worked hard for the ten previous years to get where I was. It could not get any better so there was nothing to be frightened of. There might be fifty thousand people instead of fifteen thousand watching your every move, but if you like the big occasion, the more the better.

I did find it different socially. Just as every move is noted on the field, so playing for Manchester United means that you live your life in a goldfish bowl off it. At Norwich I had been able to lead a perfectly ordinary life when away from the club. That was not the case in Manchester. The exposure that every player receives ensures that it is impossible to go into a shop or a restaurant and not be immediately recognised. If things start to go against you, such constant awareness can become suffocating. I thought it was important to throw myself into the new atmosphere immediately. We had to wait ten months for our house in Bramhall to be built, so we moved into a rented house in Wilmslow. Gordon Strachan and his wife were the first people we went out with, and gradually I became attuned to my new surroundings and my new way of life. I suppose it took four months or so before I really felt at home, but I was quietly pleased with the way things had gone.

I became a regular in the side and missed only one game in the rest of the season. In February I scored my first goal for the club when we won 2–1 against Chelsea at Stamford Bridge, but I was disappointed the following week when we lost in the FA Cup to Arsenal. Having reached the fifth round I thought there was a real chance of this team getting through to Wembley in my first season with them. It was the sort of attitude that I found myself adopting, expecting to win rather than being surprised when we did. Towards the end of the League campaign we began to play really well; we picked up twelve wins and suffered only one defeat in our final sixteen matches to finish second behind Liverpool. Ironically, that one defeat was against Norwich at Carrow Road, where I was given the inevitable roasting by the home fans. The circumstances of my transfer had leaked out. The Norwich supporters did not take too kindly to the idea that I had wanted to get away and so the chant of 'Judas, Judas' rang around Carrow Road every time I touched the ball. Nevertheless, as I finished that first season I felt I had made a contribution and felt comfortable in my new surroundings.

In August each year there was a feeling around Old Trafford that this was going to be our season. Alex Ferguson was always looking out for players who would strengthen the squad while there was never a shortage of quality players vying for places in the team. This always ensured that it would be a great occasion to play in the first team but never allowed any complacency to creep in. No matter how big an international star you might be, your place in the Manchester United team depended entirely on how well you were playing then and not how well you had played in the past.

Competition for places was as fierce as ever and expectations as high as ever when we kicked off the 1988–89 season. Our performances at the end of the previous season had been such to provide some substance to those expectations, yet once again we were to disappoint in the League. I held my place to be ever-present as we enjoyed a good defensive record. It was goal-scoring, particularly away from home, that let us down. In fact, we only won three games away from Old Trafford. That was a record equalled or bettered by the three clubs that were relegated that season – Middlesbrough, West Ham and Newcastle. To finish in mid-table in eleventh position was not what I had in mind when I left Norwich who, ironically enough, finished fourth in the League.

We were a different proposition in the Cup. Again, we had disappointed in the Littlewoods Cup. We won 6–0 on aggregate over Rotherham in our first tie, but lost 2–1 against Wimbledon in the next, with both goals being scored by a former United player, Terry Gibson. In the FA Cup, however, there was a growing feeling that we were about to justify our billing. We played out an epic saga with Queen's Park Rangers in the third round during which we drew 0–0 at Old Trafford, 2–2 after extra time at Loftus Road, and finally won 3–0 in the second replay back at Old Trafford. Oxford United came for the fourth round and were sent away with a score-line of 4–0 to consider. The fifth-round draw gave us a visit to Bournemouth where Manchester United had lost in 1984. Although we had beaten Bournemouth in the Cup the following season, the press were keen to resurrect memories of the day when the mighty cup-holders had crashed out to the Third Division side.

I have mentioned how I always enjoyed this sort of cup encounter when I was with Gillingham. The players with the small, unconsidered club are usually inspired by the big occasion. The youngsters who have what it takes use the opportunity to impress everyone with their potential. The older players summon up their resources for what might prove to be their last chance to shine in the company of the sort of players they themselves once were. In the other camp there are the household names of football. Most have come through from the lower ranks and know what to expect. Even so, it is difficult to overcome the fear of embarrassment and that nagging complacency that is made more potent by the knowledge that it can never be afforded. It is always known as the magic of the cup yet it is never magical for the big side knocked out by a minnow. It happens all too often for anyone to discount the likelihood of it happening to them.

On this occasion we were not to be one of the top sides who finish the day as the butt of every cartoonist in the country, but it was a close-run thing. Bournemouth held us to a draw of 1–1 and it was only the fact that Brian McClair took advantage of a poorly judged back-pass that we beat them in the replay at Old Trafford. Now we were in the quarter-finals, where there are no comfortable ties and the best you can hope for is a home draw. We got one, but against Nottingham Forest. I really believed that we were going all the way to Wembley, but then so did the Forest manager Brian Clough. The familiar fall-backs for journalists wanting a story at the start of any season were (i) would this be United's year for the title, and (ii) would this be the year when Brian Clough won the FA Cup. As a player and manager he had won just about every honour in the game, while a curious blank surrounded the most glamorous competition of them all. Garry Parker scored for them in the first half, while we believed we had got a perfectly good equaliser through Brian McClair. The referee, however, thought that Steve Hodge had hooked the ball clear before it had wholly crossed the line and we were out of the Cup.

Our season had virtually come to an end amid great disappointment and disillusionment. We were not going to win the League but we had honestly believed that we could pick up some silverware to reward our fanatical following. When that hope evaporated, Alex Ferguson decided that the time had come to restructure the team. Jesper Olsen had already been sold to Bordeaux, but it was after that cup tie that Gordon Strachan was allowed to go to Leeds before Paul McGrath went to Aston Villa and Norman Whiteside departed for Everton. These were quality players whose departure caused one or two questioning looks to be cast in the direction of the manager, from both inside and outside the dressing-room

Could any club afford to let such talent go? When it came to natural ability, Norman Whiteside was quite outstanding. Only twenty-four years of age when he left Old Trafford, he had crammed an outstanding career into a few short years. I must admit that I never appreciated his ability when in opposition as I did when I played in the same team. He had a reputation for being a dirty player, but his touch on the ball, for a big fellow, was quite outstanding. It was such a shame both for him and for football that a knee injury, with which he had struggled since the age of sixteen, should eventually end his career. Paul McGrath too was a superb centre-half, fantastic to play alongside. He was quick, athletic and good in the air.

If there was a shake-up of the playing staff, there was also very nearly a significant reshuffle in the boardroom. Rumours had been rife for some time that the chairman, Mr Martin Edwards, was prepared to sell his majority shareholding. At the start of the 1989–90 season it appeared that a millionaire businessman called Michael Knighton was to take over the club for twenty million pounds with another ten million being pledged for the refurbishment of the Stretford End. As well as being a businessman, he was something of a showman. None of us in the team for the first match of the new season, at home to Arsenal, will ever forget what happened just prior to the match.

Within a few weeks, Gary Pallister would have arrived from Middlesbrough to be my central defensive partner for a fee of some £2.3 million – a new record between British clubs. Paul Ince was to come from West Ham and Danny Wallace from Southampton. Neil Webb had already been signed from Nottingham Forest and was about to make his début against Arsenal, as was Mike Phelan who had followed me from Norwich. As we warmed up in the dressing-room, all feeling tense at such a time, having worked hard over the pre-season period to be ready for this moment, in burst this lively character. We could not understand what was happening when he asked the kit man, Norman Davies, for a track suit. We were flabbergasted. What was he going to do with a track suit?

What he was going to do was to go out on to the pitch in front of the Stretford End to announce his arrival at the club with a display of ball juggling. We heard the roars and watched on the closed-circuit television in utter amazement as this man, who none of us had ever met, ended his performance by smashing the ball into the goal, to the delight of the fans. If we were shocked, Alex Ferguson's face was a picture that is still vivid in my mind. 'What is happening here?' was all he could bring himself to say. He was no doubt thinking a lot more, like how such a take-over would affect the availability of funds for the new players he was lining up to bring to Old Trafford. As it happened, Mr Knighton's highly publicised manoeuvrings came to nothing and it was Carlisle United, not Manchester United, that he was to acquire.

His little bit of showmanship cannot have had too much of a bad effect on the players that day in August 1989. Perhaps it helped to relieve the tension we were all feeling because we went out to beat the defending League champions 4–1 and I scored the first goal of the season within a minute of the kick-off. This convincing win against Arsenal did not, however, signal the start of a triumphant campaign. It was not until 18th November that we recorded our sixth League victory of the season, after which we waited until 10th February to record our next success. These eleven matches without a win saw us slip down to seventeenth position in the table and things were looking decidedly glum. Remember that Alex Ferguson had made some big-money signings with players like Gary Pallister and Paul Ince coming into the side, yet relegation was becoming a distinct threat and we were out of the Littlewoods Cup. Having struggled through against Portsmouth, winning 3–2 away but being held to a goalless draw at Old Trafford, we crashed out in the next round 0–3 at home at the hands of Tottenham.

It appears quite incredible looking back now after all he has achieved at the club, but at that time the knives were out for Alex Ferguson. There was serious speculation about his future, but this was when we saw what he was really made of. The media were hounding him, but I have never seen anyone handle such a situation in the way he did. He never once blamed the players for any part of the problem. It was, by now, very much his team because he had bought most of us and had given us the chance to play for the club, so in a way he might have been entitled to allow us to take a share of the blame. That is not the sort of man he is. He did not blame bad luck either, and he might have done because in the middle of this appalling run we were drawn away to Nottingham Forest in the third round of the FA Cup. The last thing we wanted at that time was to go to meet Brian Clough's side on their own patch.

As always when we were away, I asked Janet to record *Match of the Day* for me, and watching it when I got home I heard Jimmy Hill make what I regarded as an incredible remark. While we were warming up, he said we looked a beaten team. Now I have never heard of any side who is beaten during the warm-up, but it shows what the media thought of us at that time. Fortunately, Nottingham had been taken over by Manchester United supporters that day. They gave us such encouragement during the game that a new feeling of determination came over the team. If all these people had made the effort to support a losing side, the least we could do was to fight all the way to get a decent result for them. Our 1–0 win, thanks to a goal by Mark Robins was a fight, but we scraped through.

The draw for the fourth round saw us visiting Hereford United. The way we were playing meant that we had to be candidates for one of those cup upsets when smaller clubs enjoy a moment of national glory and the big clubs suffer dire consequences. Had we lost to the Fourth Division side, I shudder to think what might have happened at Old Trafford. Along with a few others, I was unfit for this cup tie. Getting to the town itself was something of a trial because of local flooding, so it is not difficult to imagine what state the pitch at Edgar Street was in. It was a mud heap that could have been designed to embarrass a side from the top division. To add to the problems, just after half-time as one of the Hereford forwards went on a run towards goal, there was a whistle from someone in the crowd. I reckon everyone in the ground bar three people thought it was genuine. Certainly our defence was fooled into standing still, but the referee knew he had not blown and waved play on, and the Hereford forward was not going to take a chance of missing a moment of glory, so carried on. It was our immense good fortune that there was one other player on the field who did not stop. Our goalkeeper, Jim Leighton, pulled off a fantastic save. Six minutes from time Clayton Blackmore scored the goal that gave us a passage to the fifth round.

Along with most of those who had missed the Hereford tie through injury, I was fit again by the time we travelled to Newcastle for the fifth round. As a Geordie, matches at St James's Park always take on a special meaning for me. As Newcastle were at that time in the Second Division, it was a while since I had been back to play them, so this added to the sense of occasion for me. Not that anything was needed to enhance the atmosphere which, that afternoon, was quite incredible. Brian McClair had played in Glasgow derbies between Rangers and Celtic. Such matches are reckoned to be unrivalled for tribal passion, yet he claims the fifth-round FA Cup tie between Newcastle United and Manchester United in 1990 came close.

Twice we had gone in front, and twice Newcastle came back at us. Their first goal was the result of a penalty that I gave away for a foul on Mark McGhee. I was convinced that he fell over his own feet, but the referee saw it differently and the Scotsman got up himself to score from the penalty spot. Their second goal was also a little dubious in that Viv Anderson was manhandled out of the way, but again it counted. The doubt about having the required little bit of good fortune began to creep in and it took a goal by Brian McClair, set up by substitute Paul Ince, to see us through. If ever there was a typical English cup-tie, this was it. Even the Newcastle fans, disappointed though they were with the result, knew that they had seen a classic of its kind.

Our League form was no better than patchy, even if we were beginning to ease ourselves away from the immediate threat of relegation. We knew that we could not relax, but it was the FA Cup on which we concentrated our search for honours. The run had given us a certain momentum, and we looked forward to the draw for the sixth round. Surely, after three away trips, we had to get a home draw. We could not believe it when our number came up second again, with more difficult opposition at Brammall Lane against Sheffield United. Potentially, it was one of the toughest ties we could have had, with Sheffield United managed by Dave Bassett on their way to promotion from the Second Division. They were always likely to provide a stern test, but our form had started to come good at just the right time. We had got a couple of wins in the League before playing really quite well against Sheffield United. A 1–0 win might not appear too convincing, but it always became easier than that as we went a stage further than the year before and further than I had ever gone in the FA Cup before.

By now there was excitement running through the club. We were within one match of the FA Cup final, while we were doing enough in the League to quell anxieties. We felt we were turning the corner, but wanted to avoid Liverpool in the draw for the semi-finals. Second Division Oldham or First Division strugglers Crystal Palace would do us nicely. We drew Oldham, which meant that we came closer to playing at Old Trafford than at any time during our cup run. Maine Road, the home of Manchester City, was chosen as the venue because of its proximity both to Oldham and to us. Both semi-finals were played on the same Sunday to suit television, with the Liverpool-Crystal Palace tie at Villa Park taking place before our game. What a sensational match that turned out to be! It must have been the best semi-final day ever for anyone who watched both games. Crystal Palace took Liverpool into extra time and emerged as unlikely winners with a score of 4–3 with great style and excitement. Our match was to be no anti-climax.

While everyone at Maine Road or watching on television would have enjoyed the spectacle, I must admit that I did not enjoy the match. For the first time in my career I felt dreadful during the game itself. It was a steaming hot day and there was the added nervous tension associated with a semi-final. Having said that, I had played in the heat before and, by now, had experienced plenty of high-profile occasions. Perhaps it was an overdose of adrenalin, but whatever caused it, I did not know how I was going to get through the match. I could not raise a gallop. Added to this the fact that we were involved in a classic ending at 3–3 made for a quite incredible, if not totally pleasurable, experience.

If it was nerves that caused my problem, they were not settled when Oldham scored after just three minutes through Earl Barrett. It is always said that a semi-final is the hardest match to lose and here we were, so near to the FA Cup final, yet a goal down. Before half-time, however, we were back on level terms thanks to a goal by Bryan Robson. He had just come back after being out for six weeks following a hernia operation and had not even trained. Following that equaliser, another player just returning from injury, Neil Webb, scored a second. It had been something of a gamble on the part of Alex Ferguson to play both of them in a semi-final, but it had paid off. With twenty minutes to go they would have both been forced to admit that they were dead on their feet, but by then they had done their jobs. Even so, Ian Marshall equalised for Oldham. Bryan Robson was substituted by

Danny Wallace, and I will never forget the look on his face when he scored what we all thought would prove to be the winning goal. Suddenly emotions were transformed as we believed we were on our way to Wembley. Not so. Roger Palmer made it 3–3 after extra time, so it was back to Maine Road the following Wednesday evening.

It was a great relief getting through that game with our aspirations for the Cup still intact. While having a drink after the game, it transpired that others had felt as bad as I had. Our problems were behind us when we went out for the replay. At least, we thought we would be all right, but within the first five minutes a shot from Oldham crashed against the crossbar and came out. The referee saw it that way; I was not so certain that it had not gone in before bouncing out. Again, it was a great cup tie that went to extra time before we won 2–1. Brian McClair was our first scorer, Andy Ritchie equalised, and it took a great finish from Mark Robins to take us through. He had scored the all-important goal at Nottingham Forest to set us on our way and now he struck to secure our place in the final itself. The season which had been so disappointing at one time had come good at the last.

I had experienced the build-up to the League Cup final with Norwich and had gone through plenty of big games with Manchester United. The preliminaries to the FA Cup final were something else again. Any player who has not been fortunate enough to experience the thrill of preparing for what is the biggest game in domestic football has missed so much. All the media attention, all the hype that goes with it contributes to a unique atmosphere. Our preparations had been thorough, we had spent a few days away in Hertfordshire and we felt good about the match itself. Crystal Palace might not have been reckoned as a power in the land, but they had beaten Liverpool in the semi-final and were managed by a former Manchester United player in Steve Coppell who was renowned for turning out good footballing teams. It was another factor in producing a memorable occasion.

On the Friday before the game, we felt that our work was done and we could not wait for the day itself. To while away some time, I went for a walk with Bryan Robson and ended up in the local bookies'. We watched a couple of races just to while away the time. It was amazing to see the punters going in there and spotting us. I could imagine them thinking 'What are they doing here when they're due to be playing in the FA Cup final tomorrow?' We had a couple of bets on the horses and I even had a little wager on who was going to score the first goal the next day.

There was a unique buzz about the whole day when it finally arrived. I remembered John Deehan's advice about enjoying that Milk Cup final in 1985 because the day would pass so quickly if I did not absorb every moment. Those same sentiments applied now and were perhaps even more important. The Milk Cup final had been a wonderful occasion to experience, but the FA Cup final has so much tradition attached to it that it surpasses everything else. It was the sort of day that you wanted to get right. We had tried to ensure that it would go right for us by pin-pointing the strengths of Crystal Palace and working on eliminating such dangers. For instance, we reckoned that they might be dangerous from set pieces, so we spent much of our time in training perfecting ways of defending against them. We felt that if we could defend well against their corners and free kicks, we would win the Cup. They had got to the final on the strength of their well-rehearsed set pieces.

It all seems so simple on the training ground. But when you get to Wembley on the day of the FA Cup final things have a habit of not going quite as smoothly. We had been playing for about twelve minutes when Gary O'Reilly scored from a set piece! Bryan Robson got us back into the match with a header before Mark Hughes put us in front with a great goal in the second half. It was a rasping left-foot shot into the far corner. We thought we were on our way up the famous staircase to the Royal Box. That was the signal for Ian Wright to come on as a substitute in the sixty-ninth minute.

He would have been in the side as an automatic choice had it not been for the fact that he had missed most of the season because he had broken both legs. He had perhaps rushed his comeback from the second injury to get on the bench at Wembley, but now he came off the bench to stunning effect. His first touch of the ball set him on a dazzling run past four or five players before going round Jim Leighton for the equaliser.

I must admit to feeling a certain responsibility for their third goal. I left him just a little too much room as a deep cross came in from the right to allow him to put Palace into the lead only two minutes into extra time. I could have helped Jim Leighton a bit more and prevented him taking the blame for the goal. Looking back, I was probably just as much to blame as him, and possibly more so because I should not have waited for the goalkeeper to come. I should have just cleared the ball myself. I was as relieved as anyone when Mark Hughes scored his second goal with only a few minutes remaining to give us another chance in the replay. It had been an intense battle that drained the players of both sides. Even so, it is strange how little things from an epic final stick in the mind. Paul Ince had got cramp to produce one of the funniest sights at Wembley. Players frequently get cramp in one leg, but Incey managed to acquire the condition in both legs at the same time. He was still determined to continue in the game, despite trying to run with two stiff legs. It was a comical sight, watching him move about as if he had suffered an unfortunate accident. Players do get nervous in cup finals, but Manchester United players should never get so nervous that they need to wear brown shorts! Even so, he was voted Man of the Match in that final, and in the replay to follow.

To put that fact into a proper perspective, it shows how Alex Ferguson's investments were paying off. As late into the season as the cup tie against Newcastle, Paul Ince had only come on as a substitute. Now he had begun to assert himself as a key member of the side in midfield to be named as the outstanding player in two cup finals. I also believe that he has gone on from there to become one of the best midfield players in the country. If he could just complete his game by scoring a few more goals he would undoubtedly rate as one of the very best in his position in Europe. Gary Pallister had also settled into the team as a tower of strength. Although we might have been shipping a few goals, I was confident that we were building up the sort of confidence and understanding that are necessary in a successful partnership in central defence. Paul Ince and Gary Pallister were big-money buys, and cost a record £2.3 million and £2 million respectively. The surprise selection that Alex Ferguson made for the Cup final replay involved no such vast amounts of money.

We went into the replay feeling confident because we had been only a few minutes away from losing the first match. It was hard to produce an effort like that when we were out on our feet, but we had done it and we were looking forward to getting another chance. All of us except one got that second chance. The manager dropped a bombshell the night before the match when he announced that he was leaving out goalkeeper Jim Leighton to include Les Sealey who was on loan from Luton. It was a brave move, and a difficult one to make on a personal level. Jim Leighton had been a stalwart of Alex Ferguson's successful teams at Aberdeen, and had followed his manager to Old Trafford in May 1988. There had been one or two slight question marks concerning his form and he was widely blamed for the third goal scored by Crystal Palace in the first match at Wembley, even though I have admitted a certain guilt myself over that one. Looking back, even the manager might not have made the decision if he had known what effect the omission would have on the rest of Jim Leighton's career, but he could only do what he thought right for the club.

We were all shocked at the time. It is no secret that all goalkeepers have to be crazy to do the job, but Jim was a really nice lad who was liked by all the players. We all felt desperately sad for him. We were also stunned as we realised the magnitude of the decision that Alex Ferguson had made and with which he would have to live. There is no knowing what would have happened if Jim had retained his place, but it is enough to recall that the game became known as 'Sealey's Cup Final'. He made a crucial early save when the ball appeared late through the defensive wall and he somehow managed to scramble it away with his legs, and went on to completely justify his selection. He became a hero, and even now gets a special cheer from the fans when his name is read out as substitute goalkeeper. He did not have to make that many saves in the game, but he handled it well in a difficult situation.

We had played with Les in goal on only a couple of occasions, but he is not short on confidence and that rubbed off on those of us directly in front of him. He has always known that he is a good goalkeeper and would not allow any of his colleagues to be in any doubt about how he would play. Also playing in the replay was Lee Martin who had been substituted in both semi-final matches against Oldham and in the first match against Crystal Palace. This time he stayed on the field to score the only goal of the game to ensure that the FA Cup came to Old Trafford. It was the highlight of his career, for he later suffered from injuries and was replaced in the team by Denis Irwin who we signed from Oldham that summer. Les Sealey kept a clean sheet and, at the end of the match, offered his precious FA Cup-winners' medal to Jim Leighton. It was a fine gesture that endeared him to everybody. So too did the fact that he refused to sell his story. He could have made a lot of money by doing so, but kept quiet.

I had said all along that I had joined Manchester United to become a consistent winner, and now I had my first medal as a member of the team that was to provide so many more. It could be said that winning the Cup was the breakthrough needed to give us all the confidence that we were winners. It marked the start of an incredible sequence of successes of which I am proud to have been a part. The way the team was shaping, with the signings already made and more on the way to strengthen the squad, meant that we were well equipped to challenge in all competitions and to play the way Alex Ferguson wanted. He knew that the system of English football would place unrealistic demands on the players and wanted to create a squad that had quality running right through it to cope with those demands. Naturally we were elated at having achieved tangible success on that evening at Wembley Stadium in May 1990. Now we were set to ensure that the name of Manchester United would once again be revered throughout the footballing world.

The following season, 1990–91, we set out with high hopes of establishing the club in the forefront of the English game. The result achieved at Wembley the previous May had convinced us that we were good enough to succeed. Cup success was one thing, but we also wanted to end that drought in the League. Taking that ambition as a measure, it could be said that we failed. We never reached a level of consistency that allowed us to mount a sustained challenge, although we did put together a few runs that lifted us into contention. As an example, there was a period around the turn of the year when we played eight consecutive matches with five wins and three draws. We rose to fifth place in the table and were going well. If we could have continued in that form for a few more weeks, we might have gone right to the top. Unfortunately, we then played seven matches without a win, including a run of three successive defeats. That was followed by five wins and a draw in six matches, before another slump when we took one point from our last three games leaving us in sixth place. That was typical of our season.

One aspect of our League season which did please me was the fact that I finished it as joint leading scorer. It was not that we had a particularly good season in front of goal. Fifty-eight might not be a vintage year, but it was a few more than Crystal Palace who finished third in the League.

I was taking the penalties that season and managed to score seven from the spot, but there were another six in open play to ensure that I finished top of our League scorers with Brian McClair. In all first-team matches that season I scored nineteen times which has to be a good return for a centre-half, even one taking penalties. I always look to score somewhere between six and a dozen during a season so, taking away the eleven penalties, I was on target that year. My total also saw me quoted in the list for the leading goalscorers with First Division clubs – level with Gary Lineker!

Looking back at the season, our involvement in the cups probably contributed to our lack of consistency in the League. I did not score in the FA Cup as we beat Queen's Park Rangers and Bolton before we lost at Norwich. It was disappointing to lose hold of the trophy we had won in May, but we were still going well in the Rumbelows Cup, as the League Cup had become known. Our run started in the unlikely surroundings of the Shay – the home of Halifax Town. We eased past them 5–2 on aggregate, including a penalty from me in the second leg, and then I scored another from the spot as we had the satisfaction of beating Liverpool 3–1. That was followed with an even better performance when we went to Highbury and beat Arsenal 6–2. Bearing in mind the fact that Arsenal won the League that season and conceded only eighteen goals in doing so, to put six past them in one match was an outstanding performance. We were held to a 1–1 draw by Southampton in the next round, but came home to beat them 3–2 in a replay.

The semi-finals of the Rumbelows Cup came just a week after we had been knocked out of the FA Cup, so there was plenty of incentive to do well. Not that any extra incentive was really required because the opponents standing between us and another trip to Wembley were Leeds United. We beat them 2–1 in the first leg at Old Trafford, which appeared to be the slenderest of leads to take to Elland Road. I was injured for the return, but the team played superbly to win 1–0 and secure a return to Wembley. Our opponents in the final were another side from Yorkshire – Sheffield Wednesday. They were then a Second Division side, albeit one going for promotion. We were odds-on favourites to win but we failed to perform on the day. John Sheridan, Stretford-born and a lifelong Manchester United supporter, scored the only goal of the game in the thirty-seventh minute with a shot from the edge of the penalty area and I suffered one of my mercifully few disappointing trips to Wembley.

We were, however, still in the European Cup-winners' Cup and that was a competition which was to give me one of the finest experiences in football. I had been denied a chance to play in Europe when Norwich fell foul of the ban that excluded all English clubs from European competition. The ban was lifted for the 1990–91 season which meant that Manchester United qualified as FA Cup-holders. There was, therefore, added excitement in that we were once again carrying the flag into Europe as we had in the old days. There has always been a special relationship between Manchester United and European football and here was a chance to renew it. We were confident that the club was on its way back to being one of the best in the country; now we had the opportunity to measure ourselves against the best in Europe.

We were a little wary of what awaited us, but the draw was kind to us in that we started against fairly mundane opposition in the Hungarian side, Pecsi Munkas. We eased our way back into European competition with a comfortable 2–0 victory in the first leg at Old Trafford. There followed a terrible journey down to the south of Hungary where we found a pretty little town with a tiny stadium holding no more than about twelve thousand people. The atmosphere was not that of fierce competition we had been expecting. In fact, it seemed more like a pre-season friendly as we completed the encounter with a 1–0 win. That gave us a tie against the winners of the Welsh Cup, Wrexham. Without meaning any disrespect to Wrexham, we were confident of beating opposition from the Fourth Division of the Football

League over two legs. I scored a penalty in the first leg at Old Trafford where we won 3–0 and then scored in open play as we won 2–0 at the Racecourse Ground in the return.

As we moved on, the draw became a little harder. Montpellier gave us our first real test of playing in typical European competition. We were given an example of the quality of their play when held to a 1–1 draw at Old Trafford, and the French were confident of eliminating us when we went to Montpellier for the second leg. There was a hostile atmosphere with a large, noisy crowd who had been in the stadium for three hours before the game. Playing in this environment made me realise what playing in Europe was all about. I had missed the first leg owing to a broken toe, and was struggling to be fit for the away leg. To add to my problems, I had a grass burn that became infected and blew up into a lump the size of a golf ball in my groin the night before the game. The doctor and the physiotherapist did their stuff and a course of tablets did the rest. Clayton Blackmore really got hold of a free kick just before half-time and, while their goalkeeper would have been a little disappointed to be beaten, it was a fine strike. Then, just after the interval, I scored a penalty which ensured that we would have a place in the semi-finals.

Our opponents at this stage were Legia Warsaw of Poland. They played in a large stadium with a big playing surface which has staged international matches. It appeared a difficult tie in every respect. It was an open bowl and not the best of atmospheres in which to play. The regulations for European matches insist that teams are on the ground for an hour and a half before the kick-off. The somewhat Spartan dressing-rooms meant that this was not a cheerful place to spend the ninety minutes before the ninety minutes that mattered. To get away from the depressing surroundings, some of us went to wander around outside on the pitch. Lee Sharpe was among the group I was with when he was approached by his father, Leo, who was out there to watch. He had also managed to get on to what was a very good pitch. He came over to Lee, stuck his heel into the turf and said, 'It looks to me, son, as if it will take a medium stud.' Here was someone who was playing such good football that he had forced his way into the England team and who was about to play in the semi-final of a European competition being told by his father what studs to put in his boots. It was the sort of thing that probably happened in a public park every Sunday morning in Manchester, but it appeared quite comical in these circumstances.

Naturally we gave Lee a good ribbing, but the incident served two purposes. It underlined how young Lee Sharpe was and how quickly he had burst upon the scene, and it helped relieve the tension that is inevitable before such a match. We went out to win 3–1 and, again, I got my name on the score-sheet with a stunning volley from all of . . . five yards! That made the second leg at Old Trafford something of a formality and produced a strange atmosphere. Deep down we knew we had done enough to get to the final, and the supporters knew so as well. It meant that there was not the same feverish anticipation and excitement that are usually associated with a semi-final occasion. Perhaps lacking the edge we should have had, we only managed a 1–1 draw, but even that was enough to take us to the final in Rotterdam 4–2 on aggregate. Our opponents were to be the mighty Barcelona.

If our first trip into Europe to play Pecsi Munkas in Hungary had seemed unreal because of the lack of atmosphere, the setting for the final was unreal for entirely different reasons. Our supporters managed to outnumber the fans of a huge club like Barcelona by at least three to one and that was just in terms of numbers. On a decibel count there was no comparison. They had made an incredible effort to be there and were determined that we would win. It was pouring with rain, most of the Manchester United supporters were out in the open and many must have taken pneumonia back as a souvenir of Holland, but they were fantastic. When they started singing 'Land of Hope and Glory' during the warm-up, I am sure I was not alone in finding the hairs on the back of my neck standing to attention. If it was to be one of my finest experiences in football, it was also one of the most emotional.

The manager played a tactical master-stroke in his planning for that final. I have never heard of it happening before, but he decided to put our centre-forward, Brian McClair, to mark their sweeper, the great Dutchman Ronald Koeman. The idea was to stop him getting the ball so that Barcelona would not be able to play their passing game which relied so heavily on Koeman setting things up from the back. Brian did the job magnificently, and also caused problems by running at his opponent when he got the ball himself. The Dutchman might be brilliant as a distributor but is not as good as a defender. The same strategy not only cut off their source of supply but also caused them to have defensive problems. We stifled them and prevented them from playing, and it was not until the closing stages of the game that Koeman really featured. At that point he scored from a free kick, flipping it over the wall and past a disappointed Les Sealey. Les was playing with a knee which he had gashed badly at Wembley during the Rumbelows Cup final. He had been out for nearly a month and was still in a lot of pain. That presented the manager with another difficult decision, as did the composition of the midfield. He took a brave decision there in leaving out England international Neil Webb and playing Mike Phelan to give us balance wide on the right. As usual, he made the correct choices.

We had played really well in the first half without actually scoring, but we had contained Barcelona so that they were never threatening to score themselves. We felt the game was there to be won. In the sixty-eighth minute, Bryan Robson chipped the ball in from a free kick. I saw the goalkeeper, Busquets, coming and I managed to get my head on it and looped it over the goalkeeper. It was not a great contact, hitting my shoulder as much as my head, but it still took the ball over the 'keeper and was, to my mind, clearly over the line when Mark Hughes followed up like the good striker he is to make sure by smashing it further in. Most people credited Sparky with the goal, much to the displeasure of my family. They had put a bet on my scoring the first goal of the game, and lost money. Some bookmakers actually paid out on both Mark Hughes and me, but not the one where my father had placed his bet. He wrote to Ladbrokes in an attempt to get the decision reversed, but they were unmoved.

I did ask him why he had not left it alone; Mark Hughes himself was not bothered, any more than I was deep down. All that mattered was that Manchester United were on their way to rewarding all those soaking fans for making the journey. Six minutes later Mark Hughes scored another goal which was all his own and it was not until Ronald Koeman scored from his free kick ten minutes from time that we felt under pressure. I must admit that I nearly gave away a goal in the last couple of minutes when I sent an awful back-pass into the path of Laudrup. The Dane beat Les Sealey with his shot, but Clayton Blackmore was on the line to clear. Otherwise, I do not think I would ever have been allowed to come back to Manchester.

I had always considered the FA Cup final to be the highlight of my career as far as a one-off occasion was concerned, until that night in Rotterdam. I think a lot of the other members of the team shared my sentiments, with the outstanding memory being the way the United supporters had outnumbered and outshouted the supporters of a team who regularly attracted a hundred thousand spectators to a league match at home. It was a fabulous occasion that was made even more memorable by the fact that it was Barcelona who we beat in Rotterdam. We had taken over a small hotel just outside the city and after the game the party went on until about six in the morning. We had to be up again at eight and were still celebrating over breakfast.

Back home, the civic reception is part and parcel of any major success. Thousands had turned out to welcome us home from our FA Cup victory, but now there were hundreds of thousands. It took us about four and a half hours to get from the airport round the city. We were on a double-decker bus, acknowledging the cheers of the crowds and continued celebrating as we had been more or less since the final whistle in Rotterdam. There was no toilet on the bus and a lot of us were in absolute agony, trying to wave to the crowd but bursting to relieve ourselves. It was a fantastic home-coming and was fitting in that Manchester United, the first English team to win the European Cup, should be able to celebrate another European trophy in the first season in which English clubs were allowed back into Europe.

The team was now showing its true potential. The new signings had all fitted in and the younger players like Lee Sharpe were emerging as important members of the squad. We were jelling together as a formidable outfit and felt that the next season, 1991–92, had to be the one in which at last we could bring the League title back to Old Trafford to add to the other honours that were coming our way. We started off as if it would be just a formality. I think I can honestly say that before Christmas we played the best football I could possibly imagine. The level of our performance was unbelievable. Of the first twelve games we won eight and drew four. We were top of the League and could not imagine being beaten. Then we lost 3–2 to Sheffield Wednesday at Hillsborough before winning six and drawing two of our next eight matches. To go halfway through the season with just one defeat and to have forty-eight points put us in an apparently unassailable position.

Then, for some unknown reason, consistency deserted us. We began to wonder whether we could hold on, but we had put such a run together before Christmas that we thought form would be bound to return. However, as any student of football will testify, nothing can be taken for granted. We were still playing well and were still getting results, but New Year's Day began 1992 with a 4–1 defeat at home by Queen's Park Rangers. I had to miss five League matches when I suffered my longest period out of the side since arriving at Old Trafford. I had to go into hospital for a hernia operation after the condition worsened to such a point that I was forced to stop playing. I had to leave the field during a 1–1 draw at Notts County and was immediately booked in for the operation the following Thursday. There was a game against Aston Villa on the Wednesday evening and, even though I would not play, I went along to the ground for the pre-match meal and to be involved.

Earlier in the day I had gone out shopping with Janet, after which we decided to have a pub lunch. Having filled up with cheese and pickles and all the works, I went along to Old Trafford at about five o'clock. It was then that Alex Ferguson came up to me to ask how I was. I said that the hernia felt sore and was nagging away, but that I was confident I would be fine after the operation. He then told me that Paul Parker had gone down with the flu and asked how I felt about playing. Omitting to mention the plate of cheese and pickles that I had ploughed my way through a couple of hours before, I agreed to take my place in the side. We won 1–0, the hernia was wrecked that little bit more and I went into hospital the next morning to have it seen to.

As the second half of the season progressed, the matches we had been winning were all too often ending as draws, and a few more defeats began to creep into the record. We only won seven matches out of the second twenty-one, and that was not championship form. Leeds were snapping away at us, and depending on how results went on a particular Saturday, we or they would be top. The lead was changing hands regularly until Easter. That was when a backlog of fixtures caught up with us and we were forced to play five matches in ten days. There was no time to recover from injuries and players were carrying knocks from one game to another, while the mental pressure was as great as the physical.

We won the first of those games against Southampton, and drew at Luton – a result good enough to put us back

Manchester United, the winning team of the European Cup-winners' Cup, 1991.

Manchester United win the Rumbelows Cup 1992,
beating Nottingham Forest 1–0.

Bryan Robson and I hold the Premier
League Trophy in 1993.

The first Manchester United team to win the League in 26 years.

Bryan Robson (right), the late Sir Matt Busby (centre) and I, sharing a happy moment.

South Africa, summer 1993. We lost to Arsenal, but went on to beat them in the Charity Shield.

On-pitch celebrations – the road to the
1994 Premiership.

The winning team for the 1994 Premiership title.

Sharing another proud Premiership victory with Bryan Robson.

Above and opposite. Celebrating the prestigious double. One of the happiest times of my career.

Playing for Manchester United in one of our most exciting seasons yet.

on top for what turned out to be the last time that season. Then came the real turning-point, for we were beaten 2–1 at home by Nottingham Forest. We played well in the game and had lots of chances, but went behind before Brian McClair equalised. I had set up that goal by heading a centre back across goal for him, but then missed a great chance to score another myself. Considering the number of goals I had scored the previous season, this was one of the easier headers. I knew it was going to be mine all the time and perhaps I had too much time. I put it over the top. We had a photograph in the dressing-room for some time afterwards showing the despair on the faces of Alex Ferguson and Brian Kidd as I missed what was to prove a crucial opportunity. Forest went straight up to the other end for Scot Gemmill to score the winner.

We still had a game in hand as we went to West Ham for our fourth game in eight days. West Ham were already relegated and so played in a carefree spirit. A full house decided that they would treat the match as a carnival, and the West Ham players caught the mood. If this was going to be their last big occasion at Upton Park for a year or so, they were going to enjoy it. They excelled themselves and it was, ironically enough, Kenny Brown, the son of my old manager at Norwich, who scored the only goal of the game. Gary Pallister cleared a ball which struck Kenny on the knee and shot into the bottom corner from all of eighteen yards. That convinced us that the odds were stacked against us. The West Ham fans seemed to take an extraordinary delight in the fact that it was us they had beaten, while their manager, Billy Bonds, was almost apologetic as he admitted that he could not believe how well his side had played.

By this time we were one point behind Leeds and we both had two games left to play. Leeds were to kick off at twelve o'clock at Sheffield United on the day when we were to start at three o'clock against Liverpool at Anfield. All through lunch Brian Kidd was listening to events at Brammall Lane on the radio and keeping us informed. Twice Leeds went in front and twice Sheffield United got back on to level terms. In the end it was an own goal by Brian Gayle that gave Leeds a win of 3–2. They were four points clear when we kicked off, even if we now had a game in hand. It was a match we had to win, yet we knew that it was all over. Their last game was at home to Norwich and they were unlikely to lose that. That accounted for the fact that everybody on the coach going to Liverpool looked as if they were on their way to a funeral rather than a football match. It was an awful atmosphere. We lost 2–0 and it was never likely to be any other way. We felt sickened and totally drained. We had a few pints to drown our sorrows, Bryan Robson and I decided to go away for a few days, and even if the final match of the season against Tottenham was won 2–0, it was of no consolation whatsoever. We had lost the League title which we had wanted so badly and which was so nearly ours.

There had been other successes, but they did not count for much against this disappointment or the way in which we had gone out of the FA Cup and the European Cup-winners' Cup. In the FA Cup we had the satisfaction of beating Leeds at Elland Road 1–0 in the third round before going out to Southampton in the fifth. I was still recovering from my hernia operation when the team drew 0–0 away and were held to a 2–2 draw at home after extra time. The tie went to penalties and we were beaten 4–2 to become the first side from Division One to be knocked out of the Cup in such a fashion. In the Cup-winners' Cup we had beaten Athinaikos of Greece 2–0 at home after extra time after we had been held to a goalless draw in the first leg. Then we lost 3–0 to Atlético Madrid in Spain in the first leg of the next round. We actually played quite well before they scored a goal against the run of play. Two more conceded in a minute towards the end of the game virtually ended our interest in that competition. We scored an early goal back at Old Trafford which suggested that we might be able to climb out of the hole we had dug for ourselves in Madrid, but it was not to be. Atlético scored themselves and we had failed to defend the trophy we had won so gloriously against Spanish opposition in Rotterdam. However, we at least defended our record of never having lost a European tie at Old Trafford.

There was not a total lack of silverware coming to the club that year. We won the European Super Cup. As holders of the Cup-winners' Cup, we would normally have played the European Cup winners in a two-leg challenge match. However, as Yugoslavia was in such a state of turmoil, Red Star Belgrade agreed to meet us in a single match at Old Trafford which we won. Our campaign for the Rumbelows Cup had started against Cambridge with a 4–1 win on aggregate, followed by a comfortable 3–1 victory at home against Portsmouth. In the fourth round we accounted for Oldham 2–0 before we had a short run of three big matches against Leeds in the course of a fortnight. We won in the FA Cup, drew in the League and knocked them out of the Rumbelows Cup 3–1 at Elland Road. By the end of the season they probably felt we had done them a favour by taking away the distraction of cup matches to allow them to concentrate on the League. I missed the first leg of the semi-final against Middlesbrough at Ayresome Park, but I was back after the operation for the second leg. It was my first match back and proved to be the ultimate fitness test. The match was played on a glue-pot of a pitch, and it went to extra time before we won 2–1. Towards the end I felt as if my insides would drop out every time I took a step.

The final was another memorable occasion for me person-ally, in that I lifted a trophy at Wembley for the first time. Bryan Robson was injured, as was the captain of Nottingham Forest Stuart Pearce, so it was two deputies who shook hands in the centre circle before the start. It was perhaps not the greatest match ever seen on the famous turf, but a goal in the first half from Brian McClair meant that I fulfilled my boyhood dream. Every football-mad schoolboy has visions of what it must be like to lead his team up those thirty-nine steps to receive the cup. Here I was doing just that. I must admit that there was one small disappointment awaiting me at the top of the stairs. In dreams, it was someone like the Princess of Wales who stands, smiling radiantly, with the cup bedecked in red and white ribbons. When I got there, who did I find? The winner of a Rumbelows sales-incentive scheme. I am sure the girl who had been the best sales representative or whatever was a delightful girl, but she did not have quite the same aura as a member of the Royal Family!

Chapter Six

Where were you at 5.45 p.m. on Sunday, 2nd May 1993? Ask any Manchester United supporter and you will get a precise answer, because it was at that moment that we became the champions of English football for the first time since 1967. It had been a wait of twenty-six years during which frustrations had built up, hopes had been dashed and patience stretched. Now that we had been crowned as champions of the Premier League, so many dreams had been fulfilled that the moment would forever be etched in the memory of anyone who was involved with or cared for the club.

I can remember all of that marvellous day very clearly. We were due to play Blackburn on the Monday; the match was to be shown live on television and everybody thought it would decide the Championship. We were four points clear of our nearest rivals, Aston Villa, and they had a match on the Sunday, at home to lowly Oldham Athletic who needed to win all their remaining fixtures to stay up in their first season in the top flight. With Aston Villa going for the title, Oldham's chances appeared a little slim at Villa Park, to say the least. Three points for Villa would bring them to within one of us, so we would need to win the Blackburn match to secure the title.

These mathematical considerations, as well as superior goal difference, made us clear favourites. But then, we had been clear favourites twelve months earlier and had still managed to allow Leeds to come through and take the title that we thought was destined to be ours. In the knowledge of what had happened the previous year we were all a bit tense and on edge. Nobody would admit to even a fleeting thought that history could repeat itself, but deep down there was a nagging doubt that it might just all go wrong again.

So, on that fateful Sunday morning, we had gone in for a little gentle training to tone us up for the Blackburn match. We had a light lunch and then split up, with the instructions of manager Alex Ferguson still clear in our minds. He said that none of us was to watch the Aston Villa–Oldham match on television. He wanted us to concentrate solely on the Blackburn game and did not want us to be side-tracked by events at Villa Park, where he expected the home side to register a comfortable win. Always one to practise what he preaches, the Gaffer then went off to play golf with his son, Mark. At least, he might have been following his own instructions, or maybe he was just too nervous to watch the game!

In spite of his instructions to avert my eyes from the television screen I must admit that I settled down at home in front of the box to watch it all. So, too, all around Manchester, did the rest of the players. My wife, Janet, must have had her suspicions because she had spent most of the day cleaning the house, just in case anyone should happen to drop in later on. My tension and the excitement did not communicate themselves to Janet who also sat down to watch but promptly fell asleep. She was woken up midway through the first half, though, when Oldham scored. Nick Henry, who had scored only fifteen goals in his previous one hundred and seventy-eight appearances for Oldham, was the man who chose this opportune moment to record goal number sixteen and to become the toast of Manchester United fans everywhere. They had looked the better side and deserved their lead. I knew what the Villa players were going through and they never played to their form. Oldham, on the other hand, were in command, and it was not really a case of them hanging on, they just had to keep playing their football.

That goal signalled the start of the real build-up of tension. The sweat started to pour as, the longer the game went on, the more realistic our chances of winning the title became. What we were about to achieve really hit home. Janet was now wide awake and I was becoming more and more excited. For the last fifteen minutes of the game there was no chance of settling down to enjoy it as I was constantly answering the telephone. Congratulations were pouring in from all directions, even before the match had finished. A draw would have been good enough for us, but I hoped that Oldham would hang on for a win. They had done us a great favour and I wanted them to get something from the match for themselves. They did; they went on to escape from relegation. If will-power counts for anything, even from a distance, there was no doubt that Oldham would win at Villa Park, because towards the end I was kicking every ball for them myself, as were all the other Manchester United players.

As soon as the game had finished, the first of the people who might drop round arrived. Peter Schmeichel lives almost next door, Paul Ince and Paul Parker were close at hand, and gradually all the members of the team congregated at our house. We had nothing planned for Sunday evening, but by six o'clock everyone had arrived and the party was in full swing. I telephoned the manager, not just to enquire how he had got on in his game of golf, but to invite him round as well. He had a few people round at his house, too, and I remember joking with him to the effect that those of us at my house were obviously not going to get an invitation to his. Perhaps it was just as well, for by now there were some thirty or forty people lapping up the wonderful feeling that we were the champions.

It was quite a party, and even with the prospect of a match the next day or, by now, later the same day, it was not until about half-past three in the morning that the last guests departed. Bryan Robson and his wife, Denise, never did make it back to their home. They stayed over and at seven o'clock the next morning I was awoken by the jingling of glasses as the pair of them cleaned up and washed the kitchen floor. What was virtually an all-night party followed by domestic chores is a novel way for a distinguished former England captain to prepare for a match!

I am still not sure how we managed to win 3–1 against as good a side as Blackburn after a night of partying. On the other hand, we were so elated, so relieved, that we would not have found it easy to lose. The atmosphere was absolutely terrific and in all honesty that game was merely a bigger and better party than the one we had just left. This time all of Manchester seemed to be there and it certainly appeared that everyone who had ever worn the famous red shirt had come too. Legends like George Best, Bobby Charlton and Denis Law were on hand. It was their star-studded team who had last taken the title to Old Trafford and who, in a way, had made it so difficult for anyone to follow what they had achieved. However good a side was put together, it was never quite as good as the one they had adorned, at least in the imagination of the public. All these factors added to the pressure of trying to win that elusive title and, the longer our battle went on, the harder it became. Very talented teams had failed partly because the burden of expectation had proved too great. Perhaps that had even contributed to our own downfall twelve months earlier.

Whatever had happened in the past, there was no denying us our place in the club's already illustrious history. The fact that those stars from an earlier era were present on the night just added to our feeling of satisfaction. Sir Matt Busby, manager of the triumphant 1967 side and club president in 1993 was also there, beaming down on the proceedings and enjoying the cheers of the crowd. And what cheers they were! Officially the crowd numbered 40,447, but it sounded as if there could be nearer four hundred thousand, such was the vigour of their participation. The supporters had to endure the long wait just like the succession of players. The difference was that players come and go whereas supporters tend to stay with one club throughout their lives. If they had been forced by a variety of circumstances to wait twenty-six years for the title, they were determined to enjoy it now it had arrived.

I know I enjoyed it out on the pitch. Having said that, I enjoy every game I play and every aspect of being a professional footballer with a club like Manchester United. Every game is an important one, because wherever you go it is the home team's biggest match of the season with, invariably, the highest attendance. All other clubs want to beat Manchester United. That produces a special atmosphere as virtually every game is played like a cup final. All the media attention is focused on us, and that becomes the hardest thing to cope with. There is a unique intensity about life with Manchester United. There is never a game in which you can coast or relax because of the aura surrounding the club. It doesn't matter if you go to play against Stalybridge Celtic in a pre-season friendly, the place will still be packed to the rafters.

You only have to come to the training ground, the Cliff, to appreciate the following the club commands. During the school holidays in particular there are always hundreds of people hanging around just hoping to get a glimpse of their idols, let alone an autograph. Some days we have a crowd watching us train that would be the envy of many a club on the day of a match. This devotion to Manchester United is extremely rewarding. It is why I wanted to join the club in the first place but, at the same time, it is why so many people fail. They simply cannot come to terms with the magnitude of the club. My attitude has always been that I had made it to the top of my profession when I signed at Old Trafford. I was not going to worry about it but, basically, I was going to enjoy every moment.

Of course there has been the odd low moment, but in spite of that I have enjoyed myself immensely throughout my career with the Reds. What could be better than to play for what I have always believed to be the most important club in the country? If every game turns into an occasion, I was going to relish those occasions to the full. I enjoy the everyday banter of the dressing-room, I enjoy the training and I enjoy the matches themselves. I cannot imagine anything better than preparing for the game on a Saturday. That is when the adrenalin is at its peak. Old Trafford has often been described as the 'theatre of dreams' and, for me, every time I step out on to the pitch it is a dream come true. Afterwards I can sit back and analyse the game, perhaps I might have to talk about where it all went wrong, but overall I just revel in the atmosphere of playing for Manchester United.

That Monday evening against Blackburn was such an emotional occasion that I would defy anyone not to enjoy it. We wanted to win, but it was the occasion that was most significant. Things nearly went wrong when Kevin Gallacher put Blackburn one up after just eight minutes, but, midway through the first half, Ryan Giggs bent a free kick round the defensive wall for the equaliser. In the second half, Paul Ince drove us into the lead and Gary Pallister hit another free kick home in the final minute for his first goal of the season.

It was the perfect end to a wonderful day, and what followed was one of the proudest moments of my life. An hour before the game Alex Ferguson had called Bryan Robson and myself into his office to tell us that he wanted both of us to go up and collect the Championship trophy at the end of the game. Robbo was officially the club captain and, it goes without saying, when he played he skippered the side. However, his problems with injuries had meant that thirty-seven times that season I had worn the captain's armband, but I was so pleased that he got his Championship medal. After what he has done for the club, it would not have bothered me totally if he had gone up on his own to accept the trophy. Being the honest lad he is, it was Bryan Robson himself who had said to the boss that as I had been captain in the vast majority of matches he felt that I should have the honour of going up for the presentation.

That was the point at which the manager decided that we should both go. It was such a proud moment for me. If anyone had ever said that I would be captain when Manchester United won the League title and that I would be there with a fellow North Easterner to raise that trophy aloft, I would have said that they were dreaming. It meant even more to me to be there alongside Bryan because I regard him as being England's best captain of recent times and, possibly, ever. In my opinion, nobody did more for his country while he was playing and it was a great honour to stand next to him at such a moment. He had come on as a substitute in the second half which meant that he could become fully involved in the game.

Money plays an important part in professional football, but there is no money on earth that could buy a time like that. You will hear stories about players who are motivated only by finance but I can assure you that, in my experience, nobody thinks about cash when they go out on to the pitch. Certainly the financial implications of any match were never mentioned in our dressing-room. All we want from our games is success, because if we have success, we are doing our job properly. It is only when I sit down with a beer after the match or even a couple of days later that it might dawn on me that we have earned a few bob from our efforts. Being part of the team's success is all that counts.

Our dedication to winning the Championship can be gauged from our last match of the season. We had to go to Selhurst Park to play Wimbledon. Now that is never the most appealing of prospects and I think we might have been excused if, the job having been completed, we took it a bit easy and went through the motions at the end of a long, hard season. Try telling Alex Ferguson that! If anyone had dared to suggest such a notion they would have been straight out of the team.

Back in 1967 the great Championship side had won twenty-four matches, drawn twelve and lost six in their campaign. We had won twenty-three matches and had also drawn twelve and lost six. Here was our chance to match that legendary record and finally lay to rest the ghost that had haunted Old Trafford for twenty-six long years. The manager was desperate for us to play properly and to win and, anyway, it was another big occasion with a crowd of over thirty thousand. Most of them were wearing red and we were in inspired form for them. Paul Ince gave us the lead when the usually forthright Wimbledon defence failed to clear a corner. Then, to cap it all, Bryan Robson scored his first goal in the Premier League and, in spite of a late goal from Wimbledon, we had matched the record of 1966–67 in every respect. We had not scored as many goals as the old team, but we had conceded fewer and, as a defender, that pleased me.

Our start to the season had pleased neither me nor anyone else. The previous year we had come so desperately close to winning the title, only to blow up in the closing stages to allow Leeds to edge in. It had been a terrible blow, made worse by the fact that we had lost it rather than Leeds winning. Without wishing to enter too far into the realms of pseudo-psychology, perhaps, deep down, we were afraid of going through what had been a traumatic experience again. The 1992–93 season seemed to come round too quickly for us. We were just not focused enough for it to begin when it did. Whatever the reason, we got off to an appalling start to the season, and that was not just judging it by the high standards we had set ourselves.

Any club as big as Manchester United will attract its unfair share of criticism. If you are not committed to supporting them you can find no more than grudging admiration at best or, more likely, actual dislike. There are few who are indifferent to our fortunes. We knew that those who loathed us were relishing our poor start. Even those on our side were questioning the lack of activity in the transfer market. If the side had not been good enough to win in 1992, how would the sale of Mark Robins to Norwich and the acquisition of Dion Dublin from Cambridge make the crucial difference? Alex Ferguson is a canny operator, and he knew what he was about. He was also to make a significant move in the transfer market later in the season.

A league campaign is always described as a marathon, and it is usually dominated in the early weeks by sprinters without any hope of lasting the pace. Even so, when we began by losing at Sheffield United, at home to Everton, and scoring a draw at home with Ipswich, it appeared that we had been left at the start with too much ground to make up. It is always after the first three games of the season have been played that the initial league tables are published; and there we were at the bottom with just one point to show for our efforts.

I am a great believer that in football as in life you occasionally come across a little bit of luck that can trigger a drastic change in the course of events. We encountered one such in our next match at the Dell against Southampton on a Monday evening in front of the television cameras. For eighty-nine minutes it had all the makings of a goalless draw. Dion Dublin was making his début in the starting line-up and, with time running out, he scored an opportunist goal with what was virtually the last kick of the game. We were on our way with the first win of the season.

This victory had a galvanising effect on the team. We believed that we could win again in spite of the poor start and of what had happened at the end of the previous season. It set us off on a run during which we won five matches consecutively. Even so, it was a run not without cost. After going to Nottingham to beat Forest 2–0, we were at home to Crystal Palace. It was Dion Dublin's full home début and just before half-time he came out of a challenge from Palace's Welsh international defender Eric Young with a broken leg. It was a great disappointment for a lad who had settled in well with the rest of us. Just as Dion Dublin had scored late in the game against Southampton, so Mark Hughes scored a last-gasp winner against Crystal Palace.

Our next match was at home against Leeds. Games against Leeds have always been big fixtures for us. Even before the events of the previous season there was a lot of rivalry between the two clubs, and the fact that they had beaten us for the title we wanted so badly only served to intensify that feeling. They had not beaten us in the League that season, and we had drawn with them in the two domestic cup competitions, knocking them out on each occasion. Now we played them at Old Trafford and after Andrei Kanchelskis had given us the lead with a header, I had the thrill of making it 2–0. It was just before half-time when the Leeds defence failed to clear a corner that the name of Steve Bruce went on to the score-sheet for the first time in the campaign.

We completely outplayed Leeds on the day and this meant a lot to the side. With no disrespect to Leeds, we always thought that we were the better team and this win just strengthened that sentiment. We were back on our best form, and we needed to convince ourselves of the fact. It was our fourth straight victory, and we added a fifth in the return match at Goodison Park when we beat Everton 2–0. Again I got on to the score-sheet, this time from the penalty spot. This run had lifted us to third place in the League table and we had made up for our poor start to be in a position to mount a genuine challenge.

That challenge appeared to be fading away just a little as we entered another period during which we just could not secure a win. We were not beaten either, but a succession of matches in which two of the three points on offer go begging can become frustrating. It all started with our first match in the UEFA Cup when we were drawn at home in the first leg against Torpedo Moscow. A goalless draw at Old Trafford in that competition was followed by a 1–1 draw at Tottenham in the League and another goalless draw at home with Queen's Park Rangers.

When we went out to Moscow for the second leg of the UEFA Cup tie we found conditions that should have made us feel at home. It poured with rain the whole time and after another goalless draw it came down to a penalty shoot-out. We lost that 4–3 and I was one of the culprits who missed. As the regular penalty taker in the side, this was more than just an embarrassment and I was not sure how I would feel about taking spot kicks again. I did not have long to wait to find out. The next Saturday we were at Ayresome Park playing Middlesbrough in a league match and, a minute before half-time, we were awarded a penalty. Almost without thinking I stepped up, took it and scored. It was a goal that put me alongside Albert Quixall, who played for the club between 1958 and 1963, as United's leading penalty taker with seventeen.

That day on Teesside Middlesbrough came back to draw 1–1, but the following week it was Manchester United who had to stage a fight-back. We were playing another of our great rivals, Liverpool, at Old Trafford and found ourselves 2–0 down at half-time. Mark Hughes scrambled a point for us with a skilful lob in the seventy-eighth minute followed by a last-minute diving header. The run of draws continued with a goalless effort at Blackburn, before we lost 1–0 at home to Wimbledon and by the same score-line at Villa Park. That Villa defeat came just ten days after we had gone out of the Coca-Cola Cup, against by losing 1–0 at Villa Park. We had got through the previous round over two legs against Brighton, drawing 1–1 there and winning 1–0 at home.

By now we had slipped back to tenth place in the League; we had played seven League matches without a win while scoring only four goals. If you include the cup matches as well the record between 16th September and 20th November reads: played 12; won 1; lost 3; drew 8; goals 'for' 6; goals 'against' 8. The results did not display the form of potential champions. Particularly worrying was the lack of goals, but that was rectified on 21st November when we beat Oldham 3–0 at Old Trafford. It was the start of a run which took us through ten League matches without defeat, including eight victories.

During the bad run doubts had begun to creep in, as they would in such circumstances. It only took a couple of victories to lift us back into contention, but when a side is going through a sterile period like that, even the most ebullient characters can sometimes wonder from where the next victory is going to come. A similar lack of goals the previous season had been our undoing. That is not putting undue blame on our strikers, because I am a firm believer that football is a team game. Strikers will not be able to score goals unless the rest of the team is functioning in a way that creates chances. Similarly, defenders alone cannot be held responsible for goals conceded; the rest of the side has to accept a certain amount of blame for allowing the opposition enough possession to get into attacking positions. Wherever it was going wrong now, Alex Ferguson was determined to do something about it before it cost us another title.

In the week after the game against Oldham he took everyone by surprise with a signing that proved to be a master-stroke. He signed Eric Cantona from Leeds. I must admit that, at the time, I did not realise just how accomplished a player he is. I had seen him at Leeds and knew he was good, but I did not appreciate what an influence the Frenchman could exert on the rest of the team. Statistics speak for themselves: before his début with the club we had played seventeen matches and had won seven and lost four; with him in the side for twenty-one matches during the rest of the season, we lost only two and won fourteen.

Now this is not to suggest that we were a one-man team. It was just that he gave us so many options, and added that little bit of quality that we had perhaps lacked before. Successful sides often have an outstanding goalscorer who notches some thirty goals in a season. However, problems arise should that man be injured, out of form, or if he is marked out of the game. Our top scorer in league matches that season was Mark Hughes with fifteen; Brian McClair, Ryan Giggs and Eric Cantona scored nine each; Paul Ince achieved six; and even Denis Irwin and myself weighed in with five each. Another six players also scored goals in the Premier League, so opponents never knew from which direction the goals were going to come. Eric helped to create this situation by his vision; you only had to see the goals he scored himself and those with which he was involved to understand what I mean: a back-heel here, a switch of play there. Fabulous stuff that gave our whole play a new dimension.

When I said that everyone was surprised by the signing of Eric Cantona, I could be counted among those who were shocked. I suspected that there was going to be a signing, but all the talk was that David Hirst of Sheffield Wednesday was the target. When I got the call to say that we had signed the Frenchman I was absolutely flabbergasted. When he was with Leeds I had not seen him as a player who would drop into midfield to pick up the ball, spray passes about and then get on to the end of the final pass. He does this with us very successfully and emerged as a world-class player of fabulous ability.

In some clubs there is a feeling of resentment when a new player arrives, especially if he is coming into a close-knit group who have been through a lot together. There was the added consideration in Eric's case that he was arriving from Leeds and had been fairly influential in the Yorkshire club's taking the title the previous year. Problems of this nature do not tend to occur at Old Trafford. When you have been with the club for some time you are aware that there is pressure for places. It says a lot for the spirit of the club that I have never seen any resentment towards new players coming in.

I remember when I arrived in 1987 the first person to come up to me was Kevin Moran, and I was vying for his position. It was then that I realised what a terrific fellow he was. He made me feel welcome, invited me to his house, took me out for a drink and generally made me appreciate that this was a different class of individual. He introduced me to the spirit that is Manchester United and made me think that if ever I was in the same situation I should try to react with as much dignity. In fact, my place was put under pressure when we signed Paul Parker. Luckily for me, however, he slotted into the side at right back, but at the time he was a centre-half. By then I had come to understand that this was the way that Manchester United has got to be. I believe that genuinely top-class players only become available infrequently, and it is only right and proper that the best club goes for the best players when it can.

Eric's transfer went through too late for him to play in our next match, but he was watching from the stand as we went to London after the game against Oldham to beat Arsenal 1–0. He was available for the big Manchester derby match at Old Trafford, when he came on as a substitute to a rousing reception. We were two goals up against City, but then I collided with David White and, not moving very easily, I was not exactly on top of my game when Niall Quinn pulled a goal back. These derby matches are always great occasions to take part in. They do not always produce the best football, because players often get carried away with the emotion that is created by the supporters, to whom they mean so much. They are the ones who have to go into work on the Monday or to the pub that evening, they are the ones who are able to lord it if their side has won or must be prepared to take no end of stick if they have lost. The players, too, feel these matches very keenly and I have been fortunate never to have finished on the losing side in a Manchester derby. Fortunately I was not playing a few years ago when City beat us 5–1. I was injured, but I know how devastated the Reds fans felt that day.

Having secured the derby we entertained high-flying Norwich at Old Trafford. Our former player Mark Robins had been in rich goal-scoring vein to take my old club to the top of the table, and, when things were not going too well for us, there had been some criticism directed towards the manager for letting him go. However, we beat Norwich 1–0 and followed that by a draw at Chelsea where Eric Cantona scored his first goal for the club. It was not a classic by his standards, rather a simple tap in, but it was enough to take a point.

We had been 1–0 down when he struck at Stamford Bridge, but on Boxing Day we were 3–0 down against Sheffield Wednesday with only twenty-two minutes to go at Hillsborough when we came back to 3–3, with the Frenchman scoring the third goal. In fact we had been two goals down in seven minutes, with the first of them going to David Hirst who, if things had worked out just a little differently, could have been on our side in this fixture.

It said something for the character of the side that we could come back as well as we did. It gave us a tremendous boost and helped us to believe that this really could be our year. Unlike twelve months earlier, we were not way out in front and waiting for things to go wrong. Christmas is always a significant stage of the season, and we made sure ours would be a happy one by thrashing Coventry City 5–0 at Old Trafford for an impressive start to the second half of the campaign.

That left us second in the table and, after we had accounted for Bury in the third round of the FA Cup, we continued our League form with a 4–1 win against Spurs to move to the top of the table for the first time. We went to Loftus Road to play Queen's Park Rangers as leaders, just as we had been when we met them at Old Trafford on New Year's Day in 1992. Then we lost 4–1, but this time, in a game played with all the ferocity of a cup tie, we won 3–1. Mark Hughes had to go off injured and so, for the first time, we saw a front three of Kanchelskis, Giggs and Sharpe. The pace of attacks led by those three was awesome, while I remember Paul Ince scoring a spectacular goal with a bicycle kick.

We continued our interest in the last of our cup campaigns with a win over Brighton, and beat Nottingham Forest in the League to confirm our position as front-runners. Furthermore, we deserved to be there because we were playing exceptionally well and our style was being rewarded with results. We were not well clear, however, and our first defeat in ten matches at the hands of Ipswich moved us back down to second place. We went back to the top after a win against Sheffield United to avenge our defeat on the opening day of the season and then went to Leeds. The return of Eric Cantona to Elland Road lent some extra spice to an already fiery atmosphere. Those Leeds fans who only a few months previously had been chanting 'Ooh, aah, Cantona' had changed their tune. From worshipping the ground he walked on, they now showed no hesitation in spitting where he walked, and even spat at him as we got off the coach.

A return trip to Yorkshire saw us beaten in the fifth round of the FA Cup by Sheffield United and, while it is always pleasing to have a cup run, being left with nothing to play for other than the League title has its advantages. In 1992 we had played some hard cup ties and these not only prove a distraction, but they inevitably cause or aggravate injuries and produce the type of backlog of fixtures that proved so costly to us. Such sentiments were a long way from my mind when I missed a penalty in the last five minutes of that match to put us out of the Cup. The game is full of ups and downs and that was a major down for me, knowing that I had been responsible for the club missing out on a possible return to Wembley on Cup final day. It was a disappointment on a personal level and there was no respite even when I got home. My young son, Alex, who was now well into football greeted me by saying, 'Dad, what on earth have you done? How could you miss?' The upset on his face mirrored my own feelings.

Settling back to our task in the League, Ryan Giggs scored two goals in the last ten minutes of the match against Southampton after we had gone behind. One feature of the season was the emergence of our Welsh genius. That is not too strong a word to describe someone who I regard as the most skilful player I have ever seen. He is so natural and such a nice lad with it that I think he is destined for the very top of the game. He also opened the scoring in our next game, which resulted in a convincing win of 3–0 against Middlesbrough.

While we had been in cup action, our pole position had been usurped and so we were second when we went to Anfield to play a Liverpool side unaccustomed to being down near the relegation zone. The fans like us to beat Leeds, and, of course, Manchester City, but perhaps the games against Liverpool come highest on the agenda. We satisifed them and ourselves with a win of 2–1 that allowed us to return to the top of the table, but marred our record with defeat at Boundary Park against Oldham.

We were now into March and were still leading, but

we began to worry just a little as our form fell away disconcertingly. Draws followed against our nearest rivals in the League, Aston Villa, and our nearest rivals geographically, Manchester City. Another game at home to Arsenal meant that we had gone back to third after four matches without a win and there were only seven matches remaining. The next game was a crucial one at Carrow Road against Norwich, who had surprised everyone with their tenacity in clinging to the leading group. A couple of bad results and all the pundits voiced the opinion that their challenge had ended, but back they would come with qualities more usually associated with terriers than with the canaries of their nickname. At this point in the season Norwich had climbed back to the top once again and a win in this game would have put them clear in the position we wanted for ourselves.

I was going back to my former club; Mark Robins was playing against his old team-mates. The atmosphere was terrific for what was being billed as a six-point Championship decider. It was a pressurised game in which every move mattered and yet we were 3–0 up in the first twenty minutes with a display of football that rates among the best with which I have been involved in my time at the club. In spite of a consolation goal for Mark Robins, we simply slaughtered them on the night. That gave us a lot of satisfaction because we knew that March was going to be a difficult and perhaps decisive month, starting with the match against Liverpool. We had come through that and begun April in scintillating style.

Champions need many qualities of which resilience must come high on the list. The ability to dig into reserves when the going is at its toughest is a priceless asset, and we showed we had it when we played Sheffield Wednesday at Old Trafford. It was an extraordinary game. Both Viv Anderson and Chris Woods suffered injuries. I was injured, too, but the most significant stoppage came when the referee, Michael Peck, pulled a calf muscle. He could not continue and a linesman took over halfway through the match. Within a minute of

143

being in charge, he had awarded Wednesday a penalty from which John Sheridan scored. The situation remained unchanged until two minutes into injury time when I got up to a Denis Irwin corner to head the equaliser. Four minutes later, Gary Pallister crossed, the ball came off Nigel Worthington's head and I was there again with another header, although what I was doing up there at the time I have no idea! In all we played seven minutes of injury time and, while that did nothing to endear us to those who believed we had been done an unjustified favour, recordings of the match showed that there were actually ten minutes of stoppage time during the game.

In all I have scored over one hundred goals in my career, but these two gave me more satisfaction than any of the others. Nine times out of ten the first one would have missed because I had to reach the ball which was slightly behind me as I went in for it. The second I met perfectly but I did have time to think about it and, therefore, time to miss it. It came back to me afterwards how on the previous Easter Monday we had played a similar sort of game at Old Trafford when we had lost 2–1 to Nottingham Forest and I had a chance when it was 1–1. It was a simple chance and I would always back myself to score with such a header yet, that time, I missed it. Now I had scored twice to make up for that miss and the scenes of euphoria around Old Trafford showed that everyone realised we could go on to win this time.

Two days later we had to go down to Coventry to play another tricky fixture, but Denis Irwin came up trumps with the only goal of the game. Chelsea came to Old Trafford with the reputation of being our bogey side there. They had got a few good results over the years, but not this time. That set us up to go to Crystal Palace. Aston Villa, who had just enjoyed a marvellous win at Arsenal, were at Blackburn the same night and had kicked off half an hour before us. There was a buzz all around Selhurst Park as the thousands of Manchester United fans heard that Blackburn had won. Meanwhile, a cross from Eric Cantona and a spectacular volley from Mark Hughes set us on our way and Paul Ince confirmed our victory. We were four points clear with two matches to play, and that became four points clear with Villa having only one to play when they went down to Oldham on that famous Sunday.

We had gone out and taken the title by winning all of our final seven matches. We had played good football to do so and we were left with the new Premier League Trophy, a place in the European Cup and a feeling of immense satisfaction. It is a wonderful experience to go to Wembley and play in cup finals, and we had thoroughly enjoyed winning the Cup-winners' Cup when English clubs were first allowed back into European competition. However, cup competitions can be won by playing well in just a few matches during a season. Everybody involved with Manchester United wanted us to win the League title and that is what the players wanted more than anything else. To prove over forty-two games that we were the best meant everything. Along with Peter Schmeichel and Gary Pallister I had played in every one of them, while Gary and I had played in all of the cup games as well.

It is significant that there was this stability at the back. I am a firm believer in the theory that successful sides need to be founded on a stable defence. We had played together for two years and knew one another's games inside out. We were comfortable playing together. Perhaps at times our contribution goes unnoticed by the general public, but public acclaim is a two-edged sword. The forwards might get all the headlines but they attract most of the criticism for failure as well. There is a special type of pressure on a striker, in that he has to score goals to be rated as any good. Knowing that can be a heavy burden.

We had received the trophy at the Blackburn match, and had a chance to play as champions again at Wimbledon. Thousands had turned out to cheer us, as they did when we rode on an open-top bus through Manchester the following Sunday. It was a good old Manchester day, with the rain teeming down, but nothing could dampen the enthusiasm of all those who turned out to line the route. We could not go to the town hall for safety reasons but, as we went on our way from Salford to Altrincham, the fans must have been standing about twenty deep in the city centre. Incredible support. We also attended receptions given by the Mayor of Trafford and the Lord Mayor of Manchester, and in November the official club function. It took a long time to organise, but it was felt that a lot of people had contributed to the club's success and that they should all be there. In the end some four hundred and fifty from groundsmen and turnstile operators through to the president attended. It was a notable end to an unforgettable experience.

In fact, the way the people of Manchester treated us immediately after the title had been secured will never be forgotten by any of us. Whenever we went to an official function or a private party we found a really warm, welcoming atmosphere. Everyone we met would come up to us to say well done, or wanted to talk about the Championship. If I had accepted a drink from everyone who wanted to buy me one, my major fear of injury would have been sclerosis of the liver! What impressed me most was that they genuinely meant it and were as pleased as Punch that the club had won the League. Manchester was certainly the place to be for a couple of weeks.

This was in stark contrast to the previous season when Bryan Robson and I felt that we had to get away. It was not a case of ducking responsibility, it was just that everyone was so devastated by our losing the title and if you are a footballer in Manchester, there is no place to hide. You have to take it on the chin but, while that might be character-building, when you are as low as we were it is important to get out of the way and come to terms with what has happened. A few days in Tenerife sorted us out. Perhaps it says something for the players that we came back with success immediately in that momentous 1992–93 season.

Chapter Seven

When playing for a club like Manchester United, there is obviously a lot of talk about money. The Old Trafford organisation is a multi-million pound business and, as such, even the players become involved in the world of high finance. We are well paid by the standards of professional sportsmen in Britain playing a team sport, but the salaries are relatively straightforward. It is in negotiating that salary and the bonus payments, along with other commercial activities, that we are expected to behave like financial whiz kids as well as footballers.

There are some sectors of the press and the public who regard footballers as being no better than mercenaries of limited intelligence. I have always considered such sentiments to be unfair and unfounded. Top-class sport nowadays is on the fringe of show business. Some sports, such as boxing, have moved what I regard as being dangerously close to the entertainment industry. Others, like golf, tennis and athletics, have retained a secure footing in the world of sport. Football falls into the former category, namely a sport with strong ties with the entertainment industry, with the added complication of being a big money business in its own right. Which other sports clubs are quoted on the Stock Exchange?

As a rather important part of this business, it is only right that the players are rewarded accordingly. What might be termed as an 'ordinary' professional footballer, perhaps playing in the lower divisions, is still an élite performer when considered alongside all the hundreds of thousands of players who appear in organised, competitive football matches every week. Some of us have been fortunate enough to reach the top, where the hopes and fears of millions of people are invested, to say nothing of the millions of pounds that ride on virtually a single kick of the ball. We are paid proportionately more than those lower down, as is the case in any business. Having said that, I think it is fair to say that we all retain that fundamental love of the game which started us off playing football. It is an enjoyment that we share with everyone who turns out on a muddy municipal pitch on a cold, wet Sunday morning. It is where we all started and where you can still find international footballers playing when they no longer strut the premier stage. Footballers are only happy when playing football, while the money some of us earn from the game is really a bonus. It is a reward for devoting our lives to the game at which others, equally keen, have not been allowed to progress to such an extent. The same philosophy applies to all professional sport, music, drama, and even politics.

Having become a professional, every player naturally wants to progress as far up the ladder as his ability and temperament allow. The two qualities have to be considered together. Non-League football and the lower divisions are full of players who have stacks of talent but do not have the right psychological make-up to give full rein to their ability. When the chemistry is right and, all importantly, Lady Luck smiles on a player, he has the opportunity to move from club to club until he reaches the very top. Supporters will sometimes regard a footballer as being disloyal when he changes clubs. Fans do not carry their affections around the League in the same way as players do. However, they should appreciate that a footballer has a relatively short career, during which he has to do the best for himself and his family. Nobody blames a salesman when he moves from a small company to double his salary when he gets the opportunity to work for the market leader. Journalists go from local newspapers to provincial dailies to the nationals. Footballers are merely following the same career pattern.

If the aforegoing can be entered as my plea of not guilty to the charge of being a mercenary, I had better defend myself against the charge that footballers are, as a breed, of limited intelligence. I would suggest that there is as wide a spread of IQs in football as in any sector of life. I would also suggest that the public expectation of footballers takes on unrealistic proportions. Because we are good at our chosen profession, it does not follow that, by definition, we have the makings of a Nobel prize winner. Go through the ranks of professional footballers and you will find intelligence, wit, financial acumen, creative talent and all the other admirable traits. You will also find all the less desirable qualities of the human race. It is because we do not have expertise in all areas of life that we employ others to advise us and to act on our behalf. The personal manager, or agent, has been one of the growth industries associated with football in recent years.

When I went from Gillingham to Norwich, I had not become involved with an agent. It was after I had signed that first contract with Norwich and had been exposed to the world of higher finance as well as a higher standard of football that the need for an agent became more pressing. I looked to Dave Watson and Chris Woods for advice because they had more experience than me in such matters. That was when I was introduced to John Mac. He was well known in footballing circles and I was prepared to trust him implicitly. It was some time before I discovered that that trust had been misplaced, and our association ended in a court case. It has been a long and expensive campaign, but it is one that I am determined to see through in an attempt to recover the money out of which I feel cheated. My experiences should serve as a warning to others. You have to be extremely careful to whom you turn for advice.

When I transferred from Gillingham to Norwich, my salary had leapt up three or four times, and the possibility of endorsements and other commercial activities opened up for me. Then, when I came to Old Trafford, I moved to a higher plane once again. Each time it was all strange and new. When I was at Gillingham I did not have to think too hard about investments and maximising my commercial potential. Basically it was a case of living from week to week on a modest salary. There were few possibilities and, as such, there was no need to worry about investments, pensions, or anything like that. Those only became matters of concern when I began playing in the top division. That was when I needed someone to trust.

This is a subject which I have spoken about to the Professional Footballers' Association. I really believe that players need help in sorting out the good agents from the bad. There are so many around that it becomes an almost impossible task, sorting out those who can be trusted from those who cannot. Players can only work from personal recommendation, but a recommendation can be given before grounds for mistrust become evident. There is much I could say on the subject, and one day I hope to be able to do so. However, the court case is waiting to be heard and I would not want to go into detail here for fear of prejudicing the verdict.

What I can say is that when it came to signing a new contract with Manchester United, I looked elsewhere for help rather than approaching an agent. As I was involved with the PFA in sorting out the legal action against John Mac, I asked Gordon Taylor and Brendan Batson to act on my behalf when it came to negotiating my new terms of employment. I felt more comfortable with them than with anyone else with whom I had dealt. They were totally straight and forthright and there was not the haggling and bickering that often goes on at such meetings; the whole thing was completed in less than three quarters of an hour. I have suggested to the PFA that they should investigate a way in which this sort of thing could become standard practice. All players need help in contract negotiations and the PFA would be far better at offering that help than a commercial agent.

I am sure that a good agent must be worth his weight in gold, but the problem is finding such a creature. The bad ones are two-a-penny. There are plenty of stories in the game about unscrupulous agents who have managed to get themselves a slice of the action when a player moves clubs and so initiates a transfer request. The player might be quite happy where he is, but the agent makes no real money out of a contented player. He initiates the press speculation, those rumours gather pace and the agent is in a perfect position to start an auction going. I am sure that it is only the real superstars who need a personal manager. The rest of us can go to an accountant when we need financial advice or to a lawyer when we need legal help. I think there are too many agents jumping on the football bandwagon and exploiting players for their own ends.

This is not the first time that I have found myself in court. I have to admit that in my early days with Gillingham I managed to become the subject of headlines on both the front and back pages of the same edition of the local paper. During my initial season in the first team, I used to telephone Janet every day. Her family was not on the phone at the time so we arranged for her to be in a call box at an agreed time for me to ring her there. I did not like to use my landlady's telephone where I would have run up a frightening bill, so I too went out to a call box. On one occasion I had only a couple of coins available so when they ran out, I tried reversing the charges to Janet's box. It worked, so whenever I was a little short of cash I used the same trick.

It became something of a habit, to the extent that the authorities had caught on to what was happening. The practice was more widespread than I realised, because someone locally had been using a similar dodge to make calls to a box in Sunderland. Determined to find the culprit, the exchange was listening in to reversed charge calls from Gillingham to the North East to get a clue about who was making all these calls. One day I was telling Janet about being sent off during a game against Swindon and it did not take Sherlock Holmes to deduce from the newspaper reports the next day who had been making the call. When I came to make my next call, the trap had been set.

I reversed the charges, and while we were chatting I heard sirens in the distance. I remarked that there must be a fire or something in the area and carried on talking. The sirens came closer and closer and, before I realised what was happening, four police cars and a van roared up outside my telephone box. There was a moment of horrid realisation that I was the target of the manhunt. I just had time to scream to Janet 'Run, run; they've caught us!' before I was nabbed. I thought it was a bit excessive to send so many policemen to apprehend someone for making an illegal phone call costing only fifty pence, but that was before I knew that someone was doing the same thing to Sunderland and running up bills of unimaginable proportions.

Never having been in any trouble before, I was frightened. I kept saying that I was not responsible for the Sunderland calls, but they would not believe me. I was thrown into the police cells until 3a.m. when I was allowed to make a call to Bill Collins to come and get me. When I told him what I had done, he just burst out laughing. 'What a brilliant idea' was all he could say in between bouts of laughter. I was given conditional discharge and had to pay a fine. Thank goodness it appeared when I was playing for Gillingham and it did not make the national papers, because the locals had a field day. On the front page was a story headed 'Soccer Star's Shame' while the back page headline ran 'Bruce is Gill's Player of the Year'. For a little while after that the crowd chanted 'Buzby, Buzby' every time I touched the ball!

That argument with the law and the one with my former agent both had a very real basis. When it comes to the occasional disagreement with my manager at Old Trafford, Alex Ferguson, it tends to be just a minor argument over a specific issue when we both know that we are working to the same end – the good of Manchester United Football Club. We have had the odd shouting and bawling matches, but Alex himself holds that there is nothing wrong with losing your temper. However, once the dust has settled, we hold no grudges and know that it is just a slight disagreement rather than a fundamental problem. I hold him in the utmost respect, which is vital for a player towards his manager. You only have to look at what he has achieved as a manager to appreciate that he should be numbered among the very best in the business. He has also reached his position with a dignity and quiet purpose which marks him out as being rather special. I remember when he was under pressure during the 1989–90 season when things were going badly. He was under incredible duress, yet he handled it superbly and I cannot imagine anyone who could have behaved better. He always accepted the criticism even when he was not to blame. However, when the situation changed around, he was prepared to let the players take the glory. That marks out a man with special qualities that demand respect.

I have always admired Alex Ferguson's determination to succeed. In Scotland he managed to turn Aberdeen into a power, not only in Scotland but also in Europe. By doing so, he broke the stranglehold of the two Glasgow clubs and so helped bring about a great improvement in Scottish football. Now, in England, he has turned around the fortunes of Manchester United to restore the club to the pinnacle of the game. He has done so by always demanding the highest standards. I appreciated this when I made my début at Portsmouth. I thought it was a very acceptable performance to win 2–1 away from home, but the manager gave us an absolute roasting. We might have won but we did not win in the style that he insisted was right. I realised early on that he was satisfied with nothing less than perfection. Those standards are only achieved by hard work and constant effort. He arrives at the ground just after half past seven each morning, and that is after a half hour's drive from his home. Seeing this sort of dedication inspires others to strive for the same standards.

He manages to get the best out of players, as is the case with all great managers. What Alex Ferguson also has is the ability to spot talent, nurture it and then use it to the best possible effect. His critics might say that he has achieved what he has through spending power. They ignore the fact that he picked up players like Andrei Kanchelskis for £500,000, Denis Irwin for £600,000, Peter Schmeichel for £500,000 and even Eric Cantona for £1 million. These are the sort of prices which any club in the top division could afford, but they did not make the offers. Alex Ferguson did and has reaped the rewards. They have not all been big money signings. Whatever the price tag, he goes for potential which can then be developed.

I have mentioned that he has a temper, but it is only rarely seen and there is usually a good reason for it. He also has a keen sense of humour and is always approachable. If a player has a problem, he never has any hesitation in taking it to the manager. Furthermore, Alex Ferguson displays a great sense of loyalty towards his players, defending them to the last. I have seen examples of this on many occasions and it has always made an impression on me. His abilities in man management are as great as his handling of the team. Again, he has a personal involvement rather than simply having a plan and applying it in all cases.

He knows that to succeed a club has to have big resources in terms of players. He will change around the midfield and the forwards to meet certain circumstances and to give players a rest. That works well for them, but he tends to leave the defence unchanged. That suits me just fine, because I would rather keep my fitness to the required level by playing rather than just training. I share the belief that the highly skilled and creative players are permutated to give them a refreshing break and so to keep them sharp. They need to be lively both physically and mentally to enable them to do the unexpected if they are to go out and win big games with that extra little bit of flair that marks them out as being special players.

I am convinced that fatigue cost us the League title in the 1991–92 season. Fixture congestion forced us to play four important matches in just six days. With one or two players out with injuries and others carrying injuries into the matches we could not cope with what were ridiculous demands. Imagine how it would have been in the 1993–94 season if we had enjoyed a decent run in the European Cup as well as going for the domestic treble. Imagine how it would have been for the Manchester United contingent if, after that, England had been going to the World Cup in the United States. Is it any wonder that players under this type of continual pressure do not perform at their best in international competitions at the end of the season?

By having a large squad, the players who need it can be given a rest. It is not the same with defenders, however. Alex Ferguson knows me well enough to realise that I am at my best when playing week in, week out. He knows that I would not appreciate a rest and that time off could even be detrimental to my game. Such a policy also means that the defence becomes an established unit, gaining confidence and understanding as we develop alongside one another. Alex Ferguson sometimes even announces the team nowadays with a phrase like 'Playing in front of the back four in midfield today will be . . .' We take that as a great compliment, without ever letting complacency creep in. We also take great pride in keeping a clean sheet and, if some critics claim that we tend towards a defensive attitude through that, I believe that championships are won by not making silly mistakes at the back, especially in the big games. When I look back at the 1989–90 FA Cup run, it frightens me to see how many 3–2 and 3–3 score-lines we had. It must have been brilliant to watch as a paying spectator but we were giving away far too many goals. Great games, but nightmares for defenders.

I have said that strikers require different qualities from other players. They have to be able to live with the pressure on them to score goals. Defenders require another outlook on the game. We have to be able to live with the responsibility that one mistake can cost our side a championship or a cup. It is a responsibility that I enjoy. I have always responded positively to responsibility, which is why I have been named as the captain of many of the teams for which I have played. I am pleased to say the list includes Manchester United, for I regard it as an enormous privilege to be skipper of such an outstanding team. It was an honour first bestowed on me when Bryan Robson was injured during the 1989–90 season. It came as a major disappointment when, next season, I lost the captaincy to Neil Webb. Alex Ferguson called me in one day to announce that Webby was going through something of a bad patch, so he wanted to boost his confidence. He was making him captain. Such a move might have done little for my confidence, but I suppose I should have taken it as a compliment that he considered me strong enough to withstand such a blow. I was not happy, but there was nothing to be done about it. The situation did not last more than a few weeks. I was restored to the position on the night we went to Highbury in the Rumbelows Cup and beat Arsenal 6–2.

Perhaps the public at large does not understand what being captain of a football team entails. There are plenty of things that are not involved, like being privy to the manager's thoughts on tactics and team selection. Our manager keeps his thoughts very much to himself on such matters. There is a story in football which suggests that another captain who regularly wore the number four shirt might have behaved a little differently. The great Danny Blanchflower, when captain of Billy Nicholson's double-winning side at Tottenham, was considered to be more of a manager on the field than a captain. He had such an acute insight into the game that he would change tactics during the course of a match and reorganise the team without any reference to the manager. That sort of behaviour would not go down very well at Old Trafford! The nearest we have ever come to that happening was when Bryan Robson effectively dropped himself from the side during the 1992–3 Championship season. We had been playing a 4–4–2 formation with success throughout the campaign, but Robo had come off the injured list. The manager wanted him to play, considering that his experience would be vital on the run into the title. To accommodate him in the side, it meant changing to a 4–3–3 line-up. He announced such a team, but as we were showering after training, Robo said he would go to the boss to talk it through. It was a selfless move, and he convinced Alex Ferguson to pick a new side in which he did not feature, merely so that we could keep to our proven formation. There are not many players who would be prepared to sit on the bench when originally picked to play.

I regard my main function as captain as being something of a go-between, fitting in when communication is required between management and players. If Alex Ferguson wants to tell the players something, he tends to come through me, putting the captain in the position of a shop steward. With Bryan Robson around as club captain, there is another means of dealing with such matters, so that helps everyone. It also means that another of a captain's tasks, namely doing interviews and dealing with the press and media, is also spread between us. Even so, it is usually the captain of the team who is expected to provide comment after the game, so that falls to me when I am wearing the captain's armband. It takes up a bit more of my time, but I enjoy it.

There is one aspect of the job that not many members of the public will appreciate. The captain is responsible for giving out the complimentary tickets. Believe it or not, each player only gets three complimentary tickets for a game, in addition to two season tickets. Wherever we go, there is someone with a large family in that area who wants extra tickets, so I have to shuffle them around in order to keep everybody happy. If ever there was a fishes and loaves job, this is it! If all else fails, I might have to go to the manager with cap in hand pleading for a few more, but that is only in the last resort.

Despite the problems that it can cause, ticket distribution is only a minor part of the job. The main responsibility is being a spokesman for the rest of the players and a focal point when the manager deals with playing affairs. Players tend to look to the captain to act as their mouthpiece when they want an opinion expressed, or if they want something like a day off. It is the captain who has to approach the manager, providing he himself believes there is a good case to be put forward. This role of go-between is an important aspect of leadership, meaning that there is more to being captain than just calling 'heads' and then shouting encouragement to the rest of the team. The captaincy is an honour, but it is also a responsibility. I happen to relish that responsibility and regard the job as being just as much a part of my play as the actual business of performing on the field.

It is one aspect of football that is either in a player or not. You cannot train a captain. The man either has leadership qualities or he has not. I am not saying that I regard myself as having those qualities; I leave it to others to decide whether I can do the job or not. In all other areas, what is seen on the field on a Saturday is the product of what has occurred on the training ground during the week. In a typical week, on Monday morning I will drive to the training ground to arrive at about twenty to ten for a half past ten start to training. That is the time when the session begins and if you are late, you are fined. Excuses are not acceptable. I then do a few weights. Nothing too dramatic, but since having the hernia operation I have found this exercise helps to keep me in good condition. Then it is out for the training session which usually finishes at about a quarter to twelve, if we have a game coming up on the Wednesday as we so often do. We might then play a five-a-side, or do what we call a box. This is where an area is marked out and we play what is virtually piggy-in-the-middle. It is an eight against two game in which you have to keep the ball away from your opponents. This is an enjoyable relaxation after the main session which tends to concentrate more on tactics and skills rather than purely physical activities. Once the season is under way, the games become the means to physical fitness because between games we need time to rest up.

On a Tuesday before a Wednesday game, we go in and have a warm-up and perhaps not even a five-a-side. Maybe a little keep-ball session for twenty minutes or so, and that would be that. Leading up to the game, I get up in the morning and have a bit of breakfast, lounge about for a while and then go back to bed around midday. I get up again around four o'clock before reporting for the game. There is always a pre-match meal at five o'clock at the ground, consisting of pasta or chicken, soup or whatever. Diets have now become an important aspect of preparation, whereby we are encouraged to eat as much carbohydrate and as little fat as we can. All the energy intake is then burnt off during the game.

On the Thursday after a game, we go in to loosen off and have a massage, before Friday when we are preparing for a game once again. On a typical Saturday when we have a home match, we report three hours before the game for the same pre-match meal at midday. Then we go into the players' lounge to relax. The manager usually gives his team talk at half past one. This contains information about the opposition, concentrating on their strengths. He also assesses their weaknesses as a means of giving us a target to exploit. In addition, we are made fully aware of the opposition's set pieces. Free kicks and corner routines are well known to us before we go out, so we know exactly whose job it is to mark which player. He is meticulous in his preparation and must have information on every player in the game. There are probably three or four match reports made on every team before we play them. The team talk takes about twenty minutes, and then we go out for a warm-up at about half past two before the game itself begins at three.

After the match, we usually have a drink in the players' lounge, then come home to change before going out for a meal. This is when our usual League match is on a Saturday afternoon. However, because of the demands of television it is becoming increasingly unusual for this to be the case, as matches are played on Sunday afternoons or even Monday evenings. That is a pity because it means that we players have no social life at all. I always used to look forward to a Saturday evening after a game – not that I would really hit the town in a wild way, but it was good to be able to unwind by going out for a relaxed meal with Janet and a few friends. Sundays were then family days, when we would always try to go out for a family lunch, so that by the time Monday came around, I was refreshed and raring to go for another week.

I know that people will look at that schedule and claim that it adds weight to the argument for extra training sessions. It is common practice in Europe for players to spend the afternoons with their clubs as well as the mornings. There are occasions when we are called back for afternoon training, but that tends to be only as a punishment and that, happily, is rare. We will sometimes train later in the day if we are leaving for an away-match and it fits in with travel arrangements. In general the idea of physical work in the mornings and then skill practices in the afternoons would not work in this country. There are so many more games played here than on the Continent that there is simply not the time to work on individual skills to any degree. Otherwise, we would be physically exhausted. It is not possible to play two games a week and double up on training. Furthermore, the more successful a club is, the greater the demands put on the players in terms of matches, and so it becomes difficult to maintain standards.

Having said that, there are a lot of people at Manchester United who stay on a bit longer after official training. Forwards will take time to do some extra shooting practice and defenders have extra heading drills. As an example, the last one off the training ground is always Eric Cantona. People might be amazed by that as the game appears to come so easily to him, yet he is always wanting to practice his technique that little bit longer. It is not physical work, but he likes to practice his finishing by getting into different situations in which he might find himself during a match. If he has to do that, it shows what the rest of us need. We are prepared to put in the work, but it is often the case that the manager can be heard shouting from his office window to the players to come in. He is afraid of them doing too much. He appreciates the importance of rest and while the players often want to carry on training, he believes in holding that little bit in reserve.

This routine does not allow too much time for adopting new tactics. For the past couple of years we have kept largely to the same formation and style of play. These have proved to be successful and there is no point in changing merely to pander to the opposition. We believe that the way we play and the players we have can overcome that opposition. We know the pattern and it is only if we are to make a slight variation for specific circumstances that we will put on a session of functional work so that every member of the team understands exactly what is required in the new pattern. We will vary set pieces to accommodate the way the opposition plays. For instance, we were going to play against Wimbledon who, it was commonly known, would come out to catch the opposition offside if the ball was hit past the six yard box from a corner. We worked on something to counter that whereby we played it short and then crossed it in. This would stop them from coming out, and it worked. In the match we scored from a corner, which gave us all an immense sense of satisfaction.

Such a professional approach to the game is important to me. As a small boy, I always wanted to be a professional footballer and once I had become one, I wanted to reach the top of the game. I regard Manchester United as being the top, so football has become a superb way of life. To get paid, and paid well, to keep fit by doing something I enjoy so much, means that it is a first-class way of life for me. There are also the down sides to it. Every weekend is taken up for most of the year, so there is little social life to be enjoyed. When we do go out, there will inevitably be people who come up for autographs or perhaps just for a chat. In a way it is nice that they do, but it also means that I am never off duty. When I was at Gillingham, I would have loved to have been recognised. Now it is good to go away and slip into the background. Then it is possible to relax and not to worry that people are watching every move and thinking 'Should he be eating that?' or 'Fancy him drinking that'.

There have been occasions when I have managed to

go unnoticed and engage strangers in conversation about football. The summer that I left Gillingham we were on holiday and got on very well with a group of lads who were all Norwich supporters. They had no idea that I had just signed for their club and so were quite uninhibited when it came to talking about football and about Norwich. One of them said 'We've just signed a bloke called Bruce from bloody Gillingham. Who the hell is he?' We let them carry on talking for a long time before telling them that I was the bloke called Bruce. Then they would not believe me! However, they had to at the start of the season when they saw me running out in a Norwich shirt.

The fact that so many of the spectators watching us endure the necessity of working but live for Saturday afternoon means that I feel a great sense of responsibility to them. Going back to the business of being on show the whole time, it means that I feel it is important to be aware of my responsibilities so that I never let them down. When I am in the confines of my own home, I can do what I like, but outside I become a representative of Manchester United and of football as a whole. This is especially the case with children. I suppose there have been times when I have fallen down drunk in a bar, but I am pleased to say that such instances are notable for their rarity. In general I feel it is important to act with dignity and responsibility for the sake of the club and of the game. I think that is the case with most footballers. We might all get tarnished by the image of one or two who find it difficult to cope with the publicity that surrounds them, but that is a fact of life. I believe that everyone should live as they want to, so I am not one of those who becomes annoyed when someone behaves differently from me.

For me, football has to come first in the way I live my life. I know there are times when it would not be right to go to the pub for a couple of pints. I have to be aware that preparation for a match is far more important than the desire to be sociable with a few mates. It can be hard to adopt that attitude week in and week out. On the other hand, training is a routine and living becomes a routine. It can become monotonous, but on Saturday there is always something different in the game. That is the highlight, when the adrenalin starts to flow, and that makes all the sacrifices thoroughly worthwhile.

All this makes it difficult at times to keep football out of family life. I like to watch all the games that are on television, but I like to leave what has happened at the club there and not bring it all home with me. Even so, in a high profile job like mine there are bound to be encroachments on family life. For a start, there is all the time I am away from the family, while they have the same sense of being on show all the time. It becomes difficult for the children at school. It is not that they do not want to be ordinary children, but that the others do not let them. They are singled out merely because of who their father is, and they sometimes have to take a little bit of stick as well. The same applies to Janet. She is always referred to as 'Steve Bruce's wife' and seldom as a person in her own right. The only time she is allowed an identity of her own is when she is out with her friends. I am fortunate that Janet accepts the responsibilities forced on her in this respect, but there has been many a footballer's marriage that has foundered for this reason.

It also becomes difficult for us both socially to know who is a genuine friend and who merely wants to be seen in the company of a Manchester United player and his wife. Perhaps it is for this reason that we tend to have a lot more friends from the past than from the present. We keep in touch with people we knew in the North East and in Gillingham and Norwich, more than with locals in Manchester. Let's face it, nobody makes friends with a Gillingham player because he is a star! That is not to say that we do not have friends in Manchester. We have a lot, but we are always a little wary because of my position. Do they want to be my friend because they want to be my friend, or do they want to be my friend because they want a ticket for Saturday? It is not always easy to tell which category they fall into, which is why we like to get back to Newcastle and the family. You know they are not looking to stitch you up.

As well as friends in the game, it is good to have some who are not involved in football in any way. It can be refreshing to get away from football at times. That is not easy, because there are vast armies of people interested in sport and when they are, they tend to be interested in football. When the average man in the pub spends so much time talking about the game, it is natural that he wants to talk about nothing else when he is with someone who is involved in the game. He wants to know what is going on and wants to hear opinions on the current talking-point from someone close to it all. It is good to talk about other things at times, although my interests are largely sporting anyway. I love cricket and can spend hours watching the game. One of my all-time ambitions is to follow an England tour to the West Indies. That is my idea of heaven. I also like to talk to people about their jobs. I find it interesting to hear about their lives and their work. Furthermore, it is impossible to live only in the company of the team. However well we get on together as a group, there are times when we get fed up with each other. That is when friends from outside the game are necessary so that we can get away into other topics of conversation.

Invariably conversations come round to football eventually. That suits me fine, because I never tire of talking or thinking about the game. I have my own pet theories about how football could be improved. I definitely think it is important to cut down on the number of matches that are played by the top players. If you want to see first-class performances, you have to allow for first-class preparation. Athletes are not asked to peak for sixty events a year. Even horses are given time off between races to recover. Footballers are not. Furthermore, I am a great believer in summer football. As much as I love cricket, I do not think there need be a clash. I just cannot understand how spectators prefer to stand in shivering conditions watching players trying to perform on a mudheap, to sitting in shirtsleeves on a warm evening watching a game played on a good pitch. We have not got a climate which is likely to get too hot, so that should not be a problem. Furthermore, it is impossible to work on skills in training when the rain lashes down, the gale blows and muscles twang in the cold. I would rather play and train with the sun on my back.

Football has been everything to me, and I shudder to think about the way I would have spent my life had I not been fortunate enough to be taken on all those years ago at Gillingham. I suppose I would have been like so many other ordinary working men, doing a job that I did not enjoy while spending the whole week looking forward to Saturday when I could play football. It is sad that so many people are forced to live their lives in this way. If only everybody could do a job that they enjoy. It makes me realise how fortunate I have been. My regret is that this way of life is nearing an end. I still feel as fit as ever so I shall go on playing for as long as I can, but I also realise that I am nearer the end of my career than the beginning. I only wish it was still all in front of me.

I have to start thinking about what I want to do when I stop playing. I certainly want to stay in the game, because I have been involved with it all my working life. My current contract will take me through to 1998 and I am grateful to have the immediate future secured with Manchester United. When I leave Old Trafford, I do not think that I would want to go back to playing in the lower divisions, but I would love to have a crack at being a manager. That is something that appeals greatly to me, but I have to remember that there are only ninety-two such positions available, and most of them are already occupied. Another consideration is that I have experienced what I regard as being the right way of managing a football club. I would find it difficult to operate in any other way myself, but I appreciate that there are not many clubs that could offer me the opportunity to do that. It must be very frustrating to collect good players together and then be forced to sell them for the club to survive. I wanted to play at Old Trafford because of the ambition of the club, and I would need that same ambition for success in any club I managed.

I plan to help myself along this path by taking the Football Association's coaching qualifications as soon as time allows. I have been involved with running soccer schools ever since I was at Norwich. It is something I thoroughly enjoy, and something I would love to do is to take football coaching into areas where such opportunities have not been available before. It would need a sponsor to back it, but it would be marvellous to take a soccer school into inner-city areas and watch it all develop. I would like to get a sponsor involved to a degree where the kids themselves would not be charged, just to give them a chance. I had some experience of this sort of thing when we went on a tour to South Africa before the summer of 1993. I took a coaching session in a township where the skills of some of the African children were just unbelievable. If that potential can be tapped, South Africa will become a leading soccer nation. We need to develop all our own resources in this country if we want to compete.

I have got business interests outside football. I own a greetings card shop in Prestatyn in North Wales and can say that I enjoy the business world. I never thought I would get any pleasure from doing the accounts and running a business, but I find that I do to the extent that I would like to take on some more shops. I have also been involved in some media work. I have a contract to do a column for the *Today* newspaper which works well. They have only asked for football material and have never wanted what might be termed as salacious material. Perhaps they know they would not get it from me. Sky Television has called me in on occasions to comment on a game. Again, I enjoy going to a match and being involved more than I am as merely a spectator. I do go just to watch sometimes. When we have not got a game on a Saturday I take the opportunity to go to a game with my son, Alex. He is interested in football just as I was at his age. He also likes to play football during every waking moment which, again, is just the way I spent my early life. He loves it, and I get a great deal of satisfaction from watching him in matches at every opportunity. If he wants to follow me into the game I would encourage him all the way without exerting any pressure on him to do so. Who knows, one day there might be another member of the Bruce family heading for victory in football.

Chapter Eight

STEVE AS OTHERS SEE HIM
by Ralph Dellor

It was in October 1993 that I received a telephone call from a publisher for whom I had written a cricket book a couple of years earlier. He told me that his company had been offered the chance to publish Steve Bruce's autobiography and wondered whether I might be interested in helping with the project. The timing of the call amused me, because only a few weeks earlier I had met Steve Bruce for the first time. I had been covering the match between Southampton and Manchester United for BBC Television and had been asked to get an interview for *Match of the Day*. The captain of the winning team seemed a good choice and Steve obliged by coming in front of the cameras before boarding the coach back to Manchester. I was impressed with the honesty and thought that went into his answers. I realised that here I had the sort of gem that every interviewer seeks – an intelligent and articulate footballer.

What was meant to be an interview running to a maximum of two minutes went on for five. I was enjoying our conversation and he was giving interesting answers to ordinary, rather than inspired, questions. When we eventually finished, Steve went off to join the waiting coach, and I arranged for the interview to be relayed to Television Centre in London before returning home. I waited eagerly for what I considered to be an excellent interview to appear on the programme. The main match came and went. They went into the pull-together of the goals from other games, including Southampton against Manchester United. Then straight on to another match. Due to some high-level editorial whim, no part of the interview was ever transmitted. It was not an auspicious start to our professional relationship.

As we started work on this book, however, it quickly became evident how highly Steve is valued as a footballer in the game itself, even if his qualities as an interviewee had not been so greatly appreciated in Television Centre. Defenders do not necessarily attract acclaim, especially from supporters of other clubs, yet here was someone whose commitment and honest endeavour as a player earned respect wherever he went. I remember myself, as a young West Ham supporter, watching Dave Mackay playing for Spurs in the Sixties. He was no oil-painting and I winced as his tackles thundered into my heroes. There was no obvious attraction towards the player, yet how I wished he had worn a claret and blue shirt. Much the same is said of Steve Bruce. There is not a supporter in the land who would not be pleased to see him taking his place in their team's defence. That sentiment applies to managers as well. He is not, perhaps, an elegant eye-catcher. He is unlikely to go on mazy runs out of defence. There are few frills. However, managers want reliability. They want someone who will win that last-ditch tackle; who will put their head in where it matters; who will hold the defence together; and who will pop up at vital moments to snatch a goal as a bonus. These are the marks of what professionals regard as a class defender.

They were qualities spotted at an early age by his first manager at Gillingham, Gerry Summers. Earlier, he had been manager at Oxford United where he had taken on two other apprentices recommended by Peter Kirkley from Wallsend Boys – Mick Tait and Les Taylor. He knew that Kirkley was a good judge of a young player and so had no hesitation in going to Charterhouse to watch his latest protégés. There were two boys he was particularly keen on, a full back and Steve Bruce. Gillingham were quite well off for full backs, but Gerry Summers offered an apprenticeship to Steve.

He says he was impressed more than anything else by his tenacity. As a schoolboy he had a few problems because of a lack of pace and mobility. 'He took as long to turn as the Queen Mary' is Gerry Summers' description of the young Bruce. However, he was a good header of the ball and Gillingham saw him as a natural defender who was going to be a centre-half when his strength allowed it. Until that physique developed, they played him in midfield and at right back. Tottenham's Bill Nicholson used to watch him regularly and said to Gerry Summers, 'Where the hell is that Steve Bruce going to play next? He's going to be a centre-half.' Summers agreed, but his more pressing need was for an aggressive midfield player. Steve took to the role well. Perhaps, as Summers recalls, a little too well. 'He was so aggressive that he was always getting booked. I remember going to so many FA disciplinary commissions to speak on his behalf. It was all down to competitiveness – one of his great hallmarks.' Most of the bookings were for late tackles. Because he lacked pace he would arrive a little late but, being so competitive, he would go through with the tackle and end up with his name in the referee's notebook.

He made an impression by the way in which he set about proving wrong all those clubs that had turned him down before he was taken on by Gillingham. His determination got him through and what he has achieved since shows just what determination can produce.

Gerry Summers points to the fact that Steve was a model young professional. He worked hard at his game and always wanted to do a little bit of extra training and polish all aspects of his game. 'I never had any doubts that he would go on. He was doing so well in our youth side that I telephoned the England manager, Ron Greenwood, and said that if he had a better centre-half at the Under 18 level than Steve Bruce,

I would like to see him.' Ron Greenwood invited Steve to a get-together at Villa Park the following week, put him in the side, and after the youth international against Italy returned the call to Gerry Summers. 'We were murdered in Rome despite winning 1–0. We only had two players – the goalkeeper [Alan Knight of Portsmouth] and your lad.'

John Cartwright was the official manager of that England Youth team in which Steve Bruce played. He was appointed to the position at short notice when Ken Burton resigned and, knowing little about football in this age-group outside the London area, confined his first selection to those players he knew from the South-east Counties League. Of these, Steve Bruce was high on his list. 'I'd seen him play and was impressed with him, and he did absolutely magnificently. His attitude was marvellous and, although he came from one of the smaller clubs, he fitted in immediately and even showed the leadership qualities that he has today. I think he is extremely unlucky not to have had a stack of international caps because he is a good footballer and has all the attributes which are right about a player.'

Gerry Summers is proud of the fact that he played a part in helping Steve on his way and agrees with John Cartwright about his claims to further international honours. 'I think he has deserved everything he has got in the game. He should have got more, because I feel he has been unlucky not to get a full cap. I always thought they must give him a chance because he's such a difficult player to play against. Whatever else happened, in a one-against-one situation I would always want Steve involved because they would seldom get past. Steve has a great enthusiasm for football and, with that, you have always got a chance. I have seen other players with far more ability who were never going to achieve as much because they lacked Steve's commitment. If anyone doubts that, they should ask any of the strikers he's marked!'

When Gerry Summers left Gillingham, he went to do some coaching at Leicester City. However, he remembered Steve Bruce back at Gillingham and told the manager at Filbert

Street, Gordon Milne, all about him. Eventually Milne went to have a look, liked what he saw and decided to put in a bid. That was at exactly the time that Steve was on his way to Norwich. Keith Peacock was the manager who eventually sold him, but that was not until he had been in charge at Gillingham for three years. On arrival at the Priestfield Stadium he was given a dossier on all the players by Bill Collins. However, he did not want to be influenced by such reports until he had seen the players performing in the pre-season friendlies. 'It was obvious from the first match we played that he was a born winner and he helped us tremendously. He was possibly one of the best players to appear for Gillingham, if not the best. He was just superb in the air. He could also take criticism. Early on I mentioned to him about taking chances around his own area and he could accept such criticism as well if not better than any other professional I've had, without letting it affect him adversely. That is very important.'

Steve certainly lived up to the glowing report that Keith Peacock had received from Bill Collins, and that made it difficult to keep him at Gillingham. 'I was in that awkward position of wanting to keep him for the sake of the team and for my sake. I signed him on an extended contract after being there six months and he honoured that contract all the way. All through the final season I kept calling him in to see what we could offer him to stay, doing my bit as a manager, but he did all the right things. He never asked for a move but said he wanted to let his contract expire. He never made any waves to the press and did it all the right way. I sat there knowing he had to do what he had to do; I had to say what I was saying but for his benefit he had to go.'

Keith Peacock thought that there would be a mad rush to secure Steve Bruce when his contract came to an end. Teams like West Ham and Tottenham had all seen him play because the directors' box at Gillingham had been full of scouts from the big clubs. Yet the stampede for his signature did not happen. Like Steve, the manager heard the rumour about

Newcastle being interested, but no actual bid came in. He insists that he would have told Steve had there been firm interest from that direction because, in his words, he knew he would have 'hopped all the way there' if there was a chance of playing in the black and white striped shirt of his native city. It was obviously easier for the manager than the player to be patient, and he admits that the club did not tout him around because he was such an important member of the team. He was popular with the crowd and with everyone at the club, but in the end Keith Peacock was pleased that Norwich put in their offer and things worked out well.

There are players who would not have acted as honourably as Steve did, while it might be argued that he stayed too long at Gillingham. This is not a view to which Keith Peacock would subscribe. 'I feel his game matured thoroughly in his last two years at Gillingham. He made fewer mistakes and became the best player in the Third Division in my opinion. Certainly the best defender; the most swashbuckling centre-half about. If you are going to mix with the big boys you need that extra maturity. Similarly the next step of going to Norwich was probably right for him. Again, he might look back and think that he could have gone straight to Manchester United, but he might not have been quite ready for that. A few mistakes made when playing for the very best teams and you suddenly find yourself replaced by another million-pound player. I believe he had that long apprenticeship in the lower divisions which toughened his character through and through and has set him up so well now. He has been to the Halifaxes and the Chesterfields on a cold, wet January day. No doubt every time he steps on the field for Manchester United he is reminded that he doesn't want to go back there! Having said that, you can bet your life that when he was playing at Halifax he went out to play as if he was at Old Trafford.'

Having served that apprenticeship it was Ken Brown who took him to Norwich. He was pleasantly surprised that he managed to conclude the deal. He monitored him closely in the FA Cup ties against Everton where Steve was outstanding before the second replay at Gillingham. Fortunately for everyone concerned, the larger clubs backed off a little after that game in which Steve admits he did not do quite as well. Ken Brown, however, maintained his interest and eventually got his man in what he considered to be a splendid deal. 'As soon as he arrived at the club, I knew I had made a great choice because he and Dave Watson were the foundation on which we built the team. They stood by me through thick and thin, and with Chris Woods as well, it was quite a coup to have three players of such calibre.' If Ken Brown thought he had pulled off a good deal, the fact had not gone unnoticed at the Priestfield Stadium. He remembers going back there and meeting the chairman, a Mr Cox. Ken Brown was no midget, but Mr Cox was a big man by any standard. Encountering Ken Brown he picked him up off the ground, pinned him against the wall and said, 'You bloody thieving hound; you pinched our best player!' It was all in good spirit but he kept on at him throughout the match, venturing the opinion to anyone in ear-shot that Norwich had by no means paid over the odds for such a fine player.

In Ken Brown's opinion, Mr Cox was right. 'Steve had a great attitude; he was great in training. I couldn't fault him one bit. He had all-round ability while being exceptionally good in the air. He might not be the biggest centre-half but was quite fearless and gave the impression he was about six foot five the way he went for balls.' Of course, his style of play meant that he picked up the odd injury and Ken Brown recalls how he thought that Steve and Dave Watson were in some kind of race to see who could get his nose broken most often. It was courageous play that Ken Brown considers should have brought him international recognition. 'I was absolutely amazed he did not win a full cap. I still think he could get one now because age means nothing; if they can play, they can play and if they're fit, they're fit.'

Ken Brown was sacked by Norwich very shortly before Steve was transferred to Manchester United. The deal was set up because Ken Brown owed Alex Ferguson a favour. The Manchester United manager, when with Aberdeen, had put Norwich in touch with his reserve goalkeeper, Bryan Gunn. Jim Leighton, the Scottish international, was keeping Gunn out of the first team and Alex Ferguson did not want him to go to another Scottish club because he thought he would prove to be too much of an asset to a rival. He therefore asked Norwich for £100,000 and said they would never regret it. When Steve Bruce's move in the other direction was mooted, Alex Ferguson asked Ken Brown what he thought. 'You'll love him' was the answer he got. 'It pleases me that someone like Alex Ferguson regards him as being such a pro. I'm also pleased for him that he's got on so well with what is currently the best club in the country. I can't speak highly enough of him. A top-notch fella.'

Of course, Ken Brown had himself departed from Carrow Road before the transfer to Manchester United was completed. Dave Stringer was the Norwich manager who finalised the deal. Steve has made reference to the difficult circumstances in which he found himself with his new boss, but nothing that happened in those few short weeks has soured Dave Stringer's opinion of Steve Bruce. 'He was one of the players I would have liked to have kept, but obviously the die had been cast well before because Manchester United had been enquiring about him for some time. They were in the process of building the team that they have at the moment and he was, I believe, one of Alex Ferguson's first buys. Certainly he was very determined to get him and I can understand why because I was equally keen to try to keep him. Steve knew of the interest Manchester United had in him and the draw was so great that he wanted to go there. It was difficult to persuade him otherwise and, in fact, he was camped in my office virtually every day he was with me. That didn't detract from the way he performed on the pitch. He always did play his heart out when he played for us and that is the trade mark of his game. He always gives his all and never lets anything disturb him from that, whether he has problems off the pitch or not. He was a good leader in that respect because he led by example and while he was with Norwich he certainly served us very well.'

It was while with Norwich that Steve made his one and only appearance for the England 'B' team against the Maltese full international side in Valletta. His manager on that occasion was Graham Taylor who remembers an earlier association that probably even Steve himself knew nothing about. When manager at Watford, Graham Taylor travelled up to Chester with his youth team coach, Tom Walley, to watch Steve play for Gillingham. Tom Walley remembered Steve as a centre-half in the youth team and had told Graham Taylor that here was a nineteen-year-old to watch for the future. Having travelled up to Chester for an evening game specifically to watch this promising centre back, it was something of a disappointment to find Steve filling a midfield role.

Alan Hodgkinson was the assistant manager at Gillingham at that time, and some years later he was employed as a goalkeeper coach by Graham Taylor at Watford. They talked about Steve Bruce and everything said about his approach and attitude was very complimentary. By that time, however, Watford had moved on and were happy with the players they had in the middle of defence, while Steve had moved on to Norwich. Then, in 1987, Graham Taylor was asked to manage the England 'B' team when they went out to Malta. He had not long taken over at Aston Villa and had nothing to do with the selection of the side or the captain.

Steve has mentioned the feeling of disappointment when Graham Taylor announced that he had not been his choice or, indeed, he had not selected the side. This was a classic case of a misunderstanding that went unresolved until now. Graham Taylor can explain exactly what he meant by the remark into which Steve read so much. 'I wanted to emphasise to them that, from their international point of view, it was not a case of me just being brought in and then picking a team. I wanted to let all the players know that it was the England manager, Bobby Robson himself, who had selected the side and so it was very important for them to perform. If there was any misunderstanding, I am only too pleased to have the opportunity to sort it out now.'

Graham Taylor also pays tribute to the way Steve and the rest of the team played in Malta. On a very bumpy pitch which has seen the downfall of much vaunted full international opposition, the England 'B' team did well. 'It was a very, very professional performance by the entire group of players in the sort of game it is so easy to lose. I made my report to Bobby Robson and said of Steve that "he had little opposition directly against him, but he showed his usual professional appetite for the game. When forwards started to move off him he held on and kept the shape of the back four, which was very important." Bearing in mind the problems of continuity in selection for an England "B" team, the players did as much as one could reasonably expect of them.'

When Graham Taylor took over the job of England manager from Bobby Robson, Steve Bruce was still very much in the frame in international terms and had certainly not been written off. Graham Taylor acknowledges that he was unfortunate in the circumstances that prevailed. 'I think Steve Bruce has been one of those players who, given a break anywhere along the line, would probably be there with twenty, thirty or forty caps. I thought perhaps Steve might have got his break during Bobby Robson's reign, but Tony Adams went in as a youngster.

'When I took over you had a situation with Des Walker and Mark Wright and I was happy with that combination right through until 1992 when Mark Wright missed the European Championships. Then I brought in Tony Adams, choosing him as a straightforward replacement for Mark Wright because of his international experience. It was unfortunate for Steve, but one of those things. I looked at Steve Bruce on a number of occasions, but I never felt, with Walker and Wright, then Walker and Adams and Gary Pallister coming on to the scene later, that there was ever the room for Steve. But I also know that he would have never ever let me down.

A good pro. Had he been capped in Bobby's time, he might well have been ahead of the others, but when Terry Butcher retired and then injuries cropped up, I went for experience. I just happen to think he's been unfortunate. What everybody recognises with this lad is that he's had a superb career; so reliable; what a good professional and he knows the game inside out. It's all about opportunity. I think Steve Bruce was unlucky in that it didn't just fall for him.'

What he missed in international football has been compensated for on the domestic front. Rising from the relative obscurity of Gillingham to captain the most prestigious club in the land and one of the leading clubs in Europe has to represent success. When Ken Brown spoke to Alex Ferguson about Steve Bruce he said 'You'll love him'. Nothing that Alex Ferguson has encountered during the time he has been working with Steve Bruce has suggested that Ken Brown was being over-enthusiastic about his former player. The Manchester United manager sometimes comes across in public as being a slightly reticent character. He will seldom be moved from a position of equilibrium, yet he requires little prompting to expound on the qualities he sees in Steve Bruce. There is genuine appreciation of someone he obviously regards as being a first-rate professional.

'He does all the things you romanticise about in defenders. Enthusiasm; the play-with-an-injury type attitude. One of my theories about Manchester United when I came to the club was that Kevin Moran and Paul McGrath were always injured. Maybe it was bad luck, but I needed a centre back who was going to play every week. I looked at Brucey's record of playing and it was brilliant, and since he joined us I think he's missed about ten games in six or seven years. An amazing man.' Alex Ferguson also admires the way in which he has succeeded in his career. 'Some people forge careers out of the great talent they have, or by sheer enthusiasm. In looking at Steve Bruce you're looking at a fellow with a real desire to make a career out of football. And, furthermore, when he got the chance to come to United he was not going to miss it. Some people come to this club and freeze. Brucey seized the opportunity and that has got him a great career.'

Steve has himself mentioned his thoughts on that subject. The Old Trafford set-up either inspires or intimidates. He relished the chance he had been given by Alex Ferguson and was determined to repay him. He has done so to such an extent that he has been made captain. 'That speaks volumes for the relationship he has with the players and the responsibility he can take on the field and my trust in him. He's a very accommodating person, because at our club players have to do things they might not like doing, such as going to hospitals or whatever. He plays the role brilliantly and is great with kids. I'm sure he'll do well on the coaching side because he has got something to offer. He has the enthusiasm and the bubbling personality that young people love. When we were out in South Africa, he was the star attraction. All the cameras were on him coaching the kids as he gave them prizes, or made them do press-ups when they did something wrong. He had them all absolutely in his pocket; they were entranced by him.'

If that is a fine testimonial from his manager, Steve Bruce's Manchester United colleagues are equally enthusiastic about him. One of his closest associates was at Old Trafford when he arrived. Bryan Robson was not only captain of the club but also captain of England and, like Alex Ferguson, he recognised the difficulties presented by persistent injuries to the centre-halves at the club. Steve arrived and settled in immediately. 'Steve was never overawed by the place. He settled in really well with the other lads and that showed in his performances on the pitch. The big thing was that he could handle the pressure of Manchester United and the charisma that goes with it. He is very good with the media and that all helps. It always takes time for centre-halves to get a good partnership going and when he first came he was changing about with a lot of partners, but as soon as we signed Gary Pallister we began to see the best of Steve.'

Bryan Robson pays tribute to his ability to fit in socially, as well as fitting into the team. 'He's always jovial in the dressing-room and if anyone suggests going out for a pint, he's there. It's good when you've got good mixers in the club. We've roomed together for a long time, and being a couple of Geordies, I think they put him in with me when he first came because we were the only two who could understand each other! That all helps someone to settle in, but I think he fitted in because he's a good lad anyway. Part of being a successful side is that all the players get on really well and Steve's one of the best at getting everyone to mix well together. He is always talking on the pitch as well, and being good with the media all adds up to being a good captain. He does an excellent job on the pitch and is always the one who tries to gee the lads up in the dressing-room. Our success over the past few years comes from leadership on the pitch, and Steve's been a big part of that. He's an exceptionally good centre-half and we need people like him around to keep everyone else going.'

Bryan Robson mentioned the development of an understanding with Steve's partner in the middle of the Manchester United defence, Gary Pallister. He recognises the qualities that make Steve such a good team-mate and such a hard opponent to play against. 'The biggest thing Steve has going for him is his determination to win everything, not just in football but in everything he does. He wants to succeed and do well. He carries that out on to the football field. This determination is his biggest asset and it rubs off on other players. It's good, when you go into tough games, to know that you've got someone like Steve on your side.'

Watching the pair of them playing together now, you see one of the best pairings in English football. They complement one another and obviously know each other's games inside out. It was not always so, as Gary Pallister is the first to admit. 'I had been used to playing in a different way at Middlesbrough and when we first came together we did encounter some problems. However, after a bit of work on the training ground we started to get an understanding and it went from strength to strength. We've been really proud of our record over the past couple of seasons. Once you get used to people you know their strengths and weaknesses and it's possible to work round them. We've played together long enough to operate as a unit. Steve himself would be the first to say that he's not blessed with the greatest pace, but he reads the game well. And, if you put a ball there to be won, he would kill to get there. It's great for me to play alongside someone like that, knowing I can help them out or take a feed off them.'

Despite this understanding and obvious mutual respect, Steve Bruce and Gary Pallister do not always appear as a harmonious pair on the field. In fact, during a match they can become quite heated towards one another. 'We get on better off the field than we do on it, where we have had our ups and downs. We'll be at each other's throats during the match, shouting at each other but, providing we've won, we'll laugh about it afterwards. He's like an old housewife on the pitch, always ready to have a shout at somebody. I'm a bit more laid back, not believing that somebody who's made a mistake has done so deliberately. Steve appears to think you have done it on purpose. We call each other all sorts of names and swear at each other, but it is all in the heat of the battle and we forget about it when we come off the pitch.' It says a lot for the mutual respect which obviously exists between them that Steve Bruce and Gary Pallister can behave in this way on the field and yet remain the best of friends.

The same situation applies with goalkeeper Peter Schmeichel. The Bruces and the Schmeichels live within a few doors of one another to the south of Manchester, the result of the way Steve looked after the Danish goalkeeper when he first arrived at Old Trafford. It was Steve who showed him around and, once he and his family had moved in, was always on hand to help out with any problems. 'We had a very good start to our new life here and that was mainly down to Steve and his family.' Peter Schmeichel is another who is sometimes seen to be involved in shouting matches with Steve on the field. 'It is just a way to keep one another going really. There are never any hard feelings between us. People are sometimes shocked when they see the way we behave towards one another on the pitch, but we shout and shout and yet we can't hear what we're saying. He keeps our defence very solid and plays at a constant level himself all the time. You can rely on him and I think it is very much down to him that the back four play so well. He keeps a tight hand on them.'

Peter Schmeichel knew about Steve Bruce before arriving at Old Trafford. He followed Manchester United closely and knew of all the players. 'Funnily enough I was watching the European Cup-winners' Cup final just a couple of weeks before signing and remarked that Steve looked to be the typical Englishman as a centre-half who could go forward to score goals. I feel very comfortable playing behind him.' That is a fine professional testimony from the big Dane who is recognised as one of the leading goalkeepers in the world. But he goes further. 'I couldn't imagine this team without Steve Bruce in it.' There can be no higher praise for the boy who worked so hard to get into professional football with Gillingham, established himself with Norwich and, according to Peter Schmeichel, has developed into the personification of Manchester United.